D0643269

Art &
Ethnics

TRENDS IN ART EDUCATION

Consulting Editor: **Earl Linderman**
Arizona State University

ART FOR EXCEPTIONAL CHILDREN—DONALD UHLIN,
California State University, Sacramento

ALTERNATIVES FOR ART EDUCATION RESEARCH—KENNETH R. BEITTEL,
The Pennsylvania State University

**CHILDREN'S ART JUDGMENT: A CURRICULUM FOR ELEMENTARY ART
APPRECIATION**—GORDON S. PLUMMER, Associate Dean, Arts and Humanities,
State University College at Buffalo

**ART IN THE ELEMENTARY SCHOOL: DRAWING, PAINTING, AND
CREATING FOR THE CLASSROOM**—MARLENE LINDERMAN,
Arizona State University, Extension Division

EARLY CHILDHOOD ART—BARBARA HERBERHOLZ,
California State University, Sacramento
Extension Division

RELATING ART AND HUMANITIES TO THE CLASSROOM—ROBERT J. SAUNDERS,
Art Consultant
State of Connecticut

**ART AND ETHNICS: BACKGROUND FOR TEACHING YOUTH
IN A PLURALISTIC SOCIETY**—J. EUGENE GRIGSBY,
Arizona State University

709.73
G857a

Art & Ethnics

Background for Teaching Youth in a Pluralistic Society

J. Eugene Grigsby, Jr.

Arizona State University

709.73

WCB

Wm. C. Brown Company Publishers
Dubuque, Iowa

52067

Copyright © 1977 by Wm. C. Brown Company Publishers

Library of Congress Catalog Card Number: 76–12675

ISBN 0–697–03242–6

All rights reserved. No part of this publication may be reproduced,
stored in a retrieval system, or transmitted, in any form or by any
means, electronic, mechanical, photocopying, recording, or otherwise,
without the prior written permission of the publisher.

Printed in the United States of America

Contents

Illustrations

Preface

The schools of the United States are populated more and more by youth aware of their divergent ethnic backgrounds, and teachers are finding it increasingly difficult to cope with these youth who bring cultural attitudes different from those of the teachers. One example, cited in an Associated Press dispatch, concerns Samoan immigrants living in the South Bay Area of Los Angeles County, where more Samoans live than anywhere, including American Samoa. They live in a new world but have no intention of getting rid of old customs. The younger generation is moving toward fuller assimilation by marrying non-Samoans, but even the young still tend to stick together and are guided by tradition. (Several ethnic populations of the United States are larger than that of the country of origin: more Irish than in Ireland, more Jews than in Israel.) South Bay schools have recognized the need for cultural identification and build lessons around ethnic situations as much as possible.[1]

Tradition is important for understanding cultural heritage and important as a means of self-realization for youth. However, few pure traditions, which are easily identifiable, exist in the United States today. Tradition depends on generalities and keeping orderly arrangements of people and events. The art teacher must recognize and understand the importance of traditions but at the same time must not be bound by them. Creativity is stifled when neatly pigeonholed in traditional slots. Used as a background, tradition can aid in self-actualization of individuals, and stereotypes can be destroyed.

Perhaps one of the greatest stereotypes is the pigeonholing of people by color: black, brown, red, yellow, and white. This stereotype can be quickly shattered by placing a sample of color on the skin of an individual. The American Indian's description of the white man as "pink" is more visually accurate that "white." Such classification may aid in group identification, but it is destructive to individuality. The quality of the individual under the skin is far more important than any outward coloration.

June King McFee, addressing a seminar of the 1973 National Art Education Association Convention, raised the question of teacher awareness of values and attitudes between cultural groups and the awareness of differences between individuals within each group. Margaret Mead's keynote address to the 1974 National Art Education Association Convention expressed similar concerns. McFee wants to know how teachers can overcome stereotypes and see the commonalities between groups in order to see how much people are alike and how much they share the same needs, feelings, attitudes, and beliefs.

Mead feels that understanding of different cultures can complement the work of other disciplines. She writes,

> Experience of another culture can be gained by work in any society, not necessarily an isolated and technologically simple one, and, in a modern society, can complement the work of other disciplines.[2]

1. "Samoan Immigrants Cling to Tradition," *Arizona Republic*, 25 January 1975, p. B-17.
2. Margaret Mead, *Blackberry Winter: My Earlier Years* (New York: Simon and Schuster, 1972), p. 296.

McFee listed seven points dealing with attitudes and understanding, and the first one concerned a teacher's own cultural experiences and how these experiences conditioned his or her attitudes towards others.

All of us have varying strengths of stereotypes—deep seated and often built in fears, . . . We have learned a sense of ourselves which influenced how we perceived and interacted with others. We have all experienced discontinuities between our sense of self and the ways other accept, reward or reject us. These cumulative experiences strongly influence our attitudes and skills in interacting and understanding others.[3]

She suggests that insights might be gained into what students may have experienced in their own cultural group by analyzing these things in ourselves.

Another point, borrowed from her husband Malcolm McFee, an anthropologist, and from his study of Blackfeet Indians, found that people could effectively retain their old culture and effectively learn a new one.[4]

The implication of this for education, says June McFee,

is that we don't have to ask students to give up the old to learn the new . . . we can help minority group students respect and understand their own culture and still learn and cope with . . . the dominant culture.

In another of her seven points June McFee feels that any barrier to communications between student and teacher may be due to

cultural differences in values, attitudes and belief systems which must be bridged for the teacher to understand the student's background in order to create a learning situation that will have meaning.

Unless cultural differences in values and attitudes are bridged, the teacher will have a difficult time helping students grow in their own cultural art forms, to see how these have contributed to our multicultural society—and help them respond to the arts of other peoples. Surely in the arts we can be multicultural in appreciation and understanding and still retain our own unique way of working. . . .

Certainly we should not assume that a student should identify with his background culture if it no longer has meaning for him.

In a later point, McFee cites the findings of Lee Bowker,[5] from an analysis of sixty-seven American history texts printed in the 1960s. Bowker found that Indians and Blacks were in only an average of fourteen pages of text per book and much of this dealt with the so-called primitive cultures of the Indians and the Blacks as they came out of slavery. He found that they were treated as separate entities rather than as a part of the development of this country. McFee states that "self-concepts and concepts of others are developed and stereotypes reinforced through such practices."

The author feels that art teachers have many opportunities to explore the contributions of minority groups to our multicultural society and that these arts can be used in the schools, not only as arts of a given people but also as arts that contribute to the richness of the whole society. McFee cites a study by Althea Williams, which supports the contention that a minimum of examples of work by Black artists have been used in the art education texts in spite of the long tradition of fine art among Black artists.

Teachers need to be watchful that no matter how much they think they may know about other cultures, their knowledge is always subject to review and change—at the same time that cultures change, much in attitudes and beliefs do not change. Our tendency to think in progression or linearly gets in our way. Change is multidimensional and organismic—it is shifting of patterns and relationships with some new elements introduced and some parts or aspects of parts dropped. It requires

3. June King McFee, "The Importance of Affording Cultural Continuity and the Opportunity for Sharing Distinctive Cultural Patterns: Problems in a Shifting Society," in *Institute on Culturally Different,* National Art Education Association (San Diego Convention, 1973).

4. Malcom McFee, "The 150% Man in Blackfeet Acculturation," *American Anthropologist* 70 (1969):1096-1107.

5. Lee H. Bowker, "Red and Black in Contemporary Indian Texts: A Content Analysis" in *Native Americans Today: Sociological Procedures,* by Howard M. Barh et al. (New York: Harper & Row, 1972), pp. 101-111.

an openness of mind, a willingness to tolerate ambiguity at the same time that one searches for better ways to interact with individual students.[6]

June King McFee's concerns have been echoed by many art teachers. A teacher from Texas wrote,

I teach in a school made up of all Black young people whose ages range from twelve to seventeen. . . . My kids have delighted me with enthusiasm . . . we have shown up quite well in contests from here to Houston, much to the amazement of my colleagues in the "upper level," all white schools.

My problem is that I have been unable to find any materials on Art History or Art Appreciation . . . to teach these kids. In spite of their general boredom with academic subjects and their limited reading ability they are fascinated with stories I tell them about Egyptian Art and other early periods. If there were some . . . illustrated materials from which I could take excerpts, they would gain a great deal more.[7]

One of the purposes of this book is to highlight art and artists of ethnic groups that have been neglected. For this reason, greater stress has been placed on the Afro-American, American Indian, and the Spanish-speaking American, especially the Mexican-American. In chapter 2, resources are suggested for the teacher interested in pursuing information concerning arts and artists of minority groups.

Chapters 3 and 4 explore the need for art educators to understand ethnic and cultural differences between peoples and the importance of the use of models from different ethnic backgrounds to whom youth may relate. Chapter 5 explores the immigration of different populations into the United States, a migration which has established the ethnic character of different regions of the country.

The dominant society of the United States is made up of white peoples, who stem from different ethnic backgrounds. Boundary lines of these ethnic backgrounds often overlap, but they seldom melt away completely (see p. 40). Figures from the 1970 census indicate that the largest of these groups comprise fourteen percent of the total population and is a combination of English, Scottish, or Welsh origins. They are followed by Germans, twelve percent or 25.5 million of the population. The 9 million under the

Spanish heading include Mexican, Spanish, Cubans, Puerto Ricans, and people from South America. The Black population, which has been shaped into a single ethnic group (although originally as varied as the Europeans), totals 22.6 million or eleven percent in an admitted undercount, falling just below the count of the Germans. If the 30-million figure proposed by some groups as being a more accurate count is substantiated, they would exceed the 29.5 million of the English category and become the largest ethnic population. This would, on a priority based on numbers alone, suggest the need for greater inclusion in texts on the cultural heritage of this group as well as texts on art education. The case for greater stress in this book on Afro-Americans and other minority cultures is based on the need for greater information about these groups without isolating them from other ethnic groups.

At the onset of this writing, attempts were made to circumvent religious aspects of ethnic understanding. As the work took shape, the influences of religion became so apparent that chapter 6 grew into one of the largest chapters. It could have grown much larger. Time, space, and energy demanded that it be cut short, but the important points have been made. The section on Judaism has been a victim of this arbitrary decision, but I felt that the subject was much too complex to enter into in detail and that writings on Jewish religion and art are readily available. On the other hand, little is available on the so-called pagan religions, although the influence of these is likely to be greater than often realized. For this reason, information about Yoruba Orishas is included as an example of what comes under the "pagan" heading, and how such religion has had influence in the Americas.

I consider *protest* to be a *human* quality, but one with ethnic dimensions, and chapter 7 on protest has been included because of the way some minorities have used the arts as a means to creatively express protest.

6. Althea Bulls Williams, "The Social Milieu and the Black Artists in America 1900 to 1940" (Dissertation, University of Oregon, 1972).

7. Letter from a Texas high school art teacher to Bill Lockhardt, President of the National Art Education Association, 1974.

There has been no attempt to cover all dimensions of ethnic peoples as the reader will notice immediately. Not all of those under the umbrella of "minorities" have been included. The Jewish artist is mentioned only in passing. Very little attention has been given to the Oriental artist. Both of these groups have played an important role in the development of art in the United States. The role of the Jewish artist is well documented; however that of the Oriental needs more documentation. The list of artists, art critics, historians, art educators, museum directors, and collectors of art, who come from a Jewish heritage, is long and distinguished and does not require the attention given here to other lesser-known minority artists.

Chapter 8, Three Aspects of Ethnic Art, presents conclusions that I made as an observer and a student of art. Artists, teachers, historians, and critics produce, teach, and write from a point of view that accents their interest and often excludes that of others. This chapter views the spectrum of art from folk art on one end to that of intercontinental on the other, in terms of dimensions of each.

The major thrust of this book, however, is to provide information for teachers and prospective teachers so they might better understand youth from different ethnic backgrounds. It is hoped that this knowledge will aid them in helping youth develop a sense of self-respect and respect for others. It is important, however, to keep in mind that one does not live in a vacuum and that this self is developed and lives in relation to a sea of others who, in turn, have a sense of self. *Others* have their own backgrounds, their problems, and their concerns to consider; their heritage and culture have points of value that may equal or exceed the individual concerned. There is a danger in developing an overblown self-concept that is unreal, distorted, or one which requires that others be "put down" so it can rise.

The ideal situation is an equilibrium of self-respect between groups. It is hoped that we can achieve this by dissemination of information about different ethnic backgrounds. In the effort to insure youth that they are important and that their ancestors have made valuable contributions, it is also important for them to know that other people, different from themselves, have also made contributions to humanity, which can be respected and appreciated, and that each student has a contribution to make in the effort to improve the quality of living in the United States.

The writing of this volume could not have been achieved without the valuable assistance of many people. I wish to give recognition and thanks first of all to my students, who have really been my teachers and have made me aware of many points raised in the book. I wish to give appreciation to readers of the work, Grace Hampton, Deborah Beresford, Harriet Dolphin, and Rip Woods, who did far more than read for technical corrections, but who also became creatively involved and gave many valuable suggestions. My thanks goes to Bob Nash of Wm. C. Brown Company Publishers and Earl W. Linderman, the consulting editor, who extended deadlines that were impossible to meet due to teaching responsibilities. Most of all, I would like to thank my wife Thomasena, who continually encouraged, helped, and supported me while suffering through many revisions which made possible the completion of this book. Recognition must also go to my parents, who laid the foundation of my thinking about people and their worth and need to be recognized in the family of man, and to two sons, Eugene and Marshall, who through confidence and gentle urging played an important role in completing this volume.

1 Foundations of Ethnic Art in a Pluralistic Society

The subject of this book, *Art ana Ethics,* had its genesis in a presentation made at the Pacific Arts Association Convention in Portland, Oregon, titled "Paint The Invisible Artist Black, Brown and Red." The purpose of this presentation was to provide information about artists of these ethnic backgrounds and hopefully to encourage students and teachers to become more curious about them—a curiosity that would lead to the discovery of the rich cultural and visual variations to be found in the works of these artists as well as in the story of their struggle to achieve recognition. Sources of information were given to aid teachers of the White majority culture to relate to youth from Black, Brown, and Red minority cultures.

The year 1970 saw a slackening of the turbulent 1960s when violent clashes, riots, and burning of inner cities gave dramatic evidence of dissatisfaction of minorities, particularly Blacks, who comprised the largest, most vocal and visible minority population of the United States. The Brown peoples, comprised of Mexican-American, Puerto-Rican, and other Spanish-speaking populations, followed by native American Indians, had begun to be more vocal about their dissatisfaction with the lack of "all deliberate speed" in implementing the 1954 Supreme Court decision or subsequent civil rights enactments passed by Congress to improve the quality of living for minority and poor people. Although violence slacked off by 1970, the urgency for change remained, and much of the action moved from the street into the schools. It is not surprising that in schools the art room was often the place of the least friction. There were reasons for this lack of friction. Two important

ones, cited by Dr. Charles Murray, an associate high school principal in Phoenix, Arizona, were the opportunity for self-expression and for cultural identity. The two are closely related, but the second, building a strong self-image, is greatly reinforced when viable models are available to emulate. All art rooms did not escape some forms of violence as opportunities for self-realization were not always available. A dormant form of violence is in the negative form of apathy.

The presentation at the Portland conference was for the purpose of showing works by successful Black, Brown, and Red artists and of telling something of their backgrounds. By doing this, art teachers in attendance, who were mostly of the White majority population, could have information to build better relations with youth of different cultures and to provide models with whom they could relate.

The purpose of this text will vary somewhat from that of the Portland presentation and will be directed more to probing factors and asking questions concerning various ethnic populations and art. Questions will be asked such as who are the ethnics and what are the components of arts that identify them as ethnic, what art is ethnic and what art is nonethnic, and who are the ethnic artists? My editorial answers will be given from a personal point of view, which may or may not always be that of the reader.

The overall view of ethnics presented here considers the flow of world populations into the United States from its discovery by Columbus until the present. The focus of this view is on those people generally considered as minority ethnic populations—Blacks, native American Indians, and the Spanish speaking—

Figure 1.1 Alan Houser. *Fresh Trail, Apache War Party*. From the collection of the Heard Museum, Phoenix, Arizona.

as opposed to ethnic components of the majority White population, which are normally included in texts on art. Such limitations are necessary because of space and time and also because these three segments of the population present problems that the classroom art teacher is least prepared to cope with. Art teachers with a better understanding of ethnic backgrounds and artistic heritage and with knowledge of contemporary contributions of artists from these backgrounds may be better able to devise strategies for more effective teaching of youth from these backgrounds. Effective strategies for reaching these youth may serve as a basis for methods of teaching youth from other ethnic segments of the population not so easily identified as the Black, Indian, and Chicano.

The shift in emphasis from the Portland conference presentation is mainly because material, concerning the artists, their works, philosophies and lives, is now more available. At the time of that conference few examples of works by contemporary artists of these ethnic backgrounds were readily available to the average classroom teacher. There has been an increase in the publication of monographs, books, and exhibit catalogs devoted to individuals or groups of minority ethnic artists, but few of their works are to be found in texts on art education or art history in general use in schools and colleges, with some notable exceptions. The following chapter is concerned with selected references about Black, Indian, and Chicano artists from books, exhibit catalogs, slide collections, journals, and newspaper articles.

Figure 1.2 Michio Kobayashi. Conference Symbol. From the program of the Celebration of the Peoples, NAEA Regional Conference.

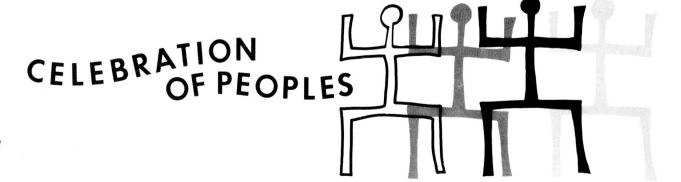

CELEBRATION OF PEOPLES

2 Ethnic Resource Materials for Art Educators

The Black/Negro/Afro-American Artists

One of the earliest books to discuss the Afro-American artist was by Alain Locke, *The Negro in Art*, published by the Associates in Negro Folk Education in 1940. This was possibly first compiled four years earlier as a study booklet for Locke's humanities and art students. Locke was a philosophy teacher at Howard University with special interest in aesthetics and African art. He contributed articles on these subjects to many of the leading art journals. He is particularly known for his anthology, *The New Negro*, which deals with writers of the Harlem Renaissance.

James Porter, a colleague of Locke at Howard, wrote *Modern Negro Art*, published by the Dryden Press in 1943 and reprinted in 1969. This was a definitive book, better known than Locke's work because it was more readily available and until the early 1970s was considered to be the most important book about Afro-American artists. It is important to note that both Locke and Porter were members of the ethnic community that they wrote about. Cedric Dover, an Englishman, brought another dimension of observation in his *American Negro Art* published in 1960. Dover's book updated the work of Porter and introduced many new artists, who had become active in the seventeen years since Porter's work was first published. It had many more illustrations, some in color, and a larger format than that of Porter's. Some argue that the critical analyses made by Dover fall short of those by Porter, and many of the artists strongly objected to the manner in which Dover presented them and their works. Still this volume made its contributions as it was one of the few books at the time dealing with the subject of the Negro artist. It was not until 1969 that Samella Lewis and Ruth Waddy published the first of two volumes of *Black Artists on Art*. These volumes, the second one published in 1971, differ from the Porter and Dover books in that they present comments by the artists and reproductions of their works. The decade of the 1970s has already seen the publication of a number of books dealing with the Black or Afro-American artist. In 1971 Dodd, Mead & Company published *17 Black Artists* by Elton Fax, and Van Nostrand Reinhold Company published Judith Wragg Chase's *Afro-American Art and Craft*. *The Afro-American Artist* by Elsa Honig Fine was published by Holt, Rinehart and Winston, Inc., in 1973. Several other books dealing with Black artists are due for publication, and the problems teachers have had in obtaining material on Black artists is no longer as acute as it has been, although little of it has found its way into the classroom art textbook as yet.

In spite of the fact that there were few books on Black artists published before the 1970s, there were a number of articles on the subject in professional journals, magazines, and newspapers. Most notable among these is the art section of *Ebony* in the "Emancipation Proclamation Centennial" issue of September 1963. In February 1968, *Ebony* reviewed the exhibit, Afro-American Art 1800-1950, produced for New York City University by Romare Bearden and Carroll Greene, Jr. *The Art Gallery Magazine* published an article on Black artists by Carroll Greene in 1968 and a follow-up in 1970. *Humble Way,* a publication of the Humble Oil Company, devoted a section to the Afro-American artist written by Greene. Other magazines, *Fortune, Playboy,* and *Crisis* to mention a few, have carried articles and illustrations of works by and about Black artists. Henry O. Tanner, Hale Woodruff, Jacob Lawrence, Romare Bearden, Charles White, Richard Hunt, Sam Gilliam, Charles Alston, John Biggers, Elizabeth Catlett, Alma Thomas, Aaron Douglas, Meta Warrick Fuller, William H. Johnson, Sargent Johnson, Elton Fax, Augusta Savage, Horace Pippin, Selma Burke, and Joshua Johnston are only a few artists of African heritage, who have become known to that public interested in the Black artist. A section of July 18, 1970 *Saturday Review,* titled "Black Arts for Black Youth," illustrated the importance of Black artists as models for Black youth and described several schools with programs attempting to meet this need.

Exhibition catalogs have provided a valuable source of information about ethnic artists, although these catalogs are not as readily available as books and periodicals. The Harmon Foundation pioneered in developing exhibitions of works by Black artists as early as the second decade of this century. The WPA Federal Art Project provided opportunity for artists of different ethnic backgrounds to exhibit their works during the 1930s and early 1940s. Seldom were artists of these exhibits identified ethnically unless the exhibit was limited to a particular ethnic group.[1]

A major exhibit was assembled by the American Negro Exposition in 1940 titled The Art of the American Negro (1851-1940) and held at the Tanner Art Galleries in Chicago. A lithograph by Charles White, reproduced on the cover of the catalog, was one of over four hundred works included. Listed by title were 316 of these, another group by children was on loan from the Federal Art Project, and an impressive collection of African art came from several collections. A series of forty-one paintings by Jacob Lawrence on the life of Toussaint L'Ouverture was listed under a single title. A memorial section included works by Robert Duncanson (1821-1871), Edward Bannister (1828-1901), Edwin Harleston (1882-1931), and Henry O. Tanner (1859-1937) along with others. The major section was devoted to contemporary artists, many of whom have since become well known, including Romare Bearden, Hale Woodruff, Robert Blackburn, Rex Gorleigh, Ernie Crichlow, Elton Fax, Hughie Lee-Smith, Norman Lewis, Selma Burke, Elizabeth Catlett, Richmond Barthe, William Artis, Beauford Delaney, to mention some of over one hundred artists exhibiting. Alaine Locke wrote the introduction to the catalog and congratulated the authorities of the Exposition on "assembling the most comprehensive and representative collection of the Negro's art that has ever been presented to public view."

In 1945 the Albany Institute of History and Art produced an exhibit, The Negro Artist Comes of Age, and again Locke contributed to the catalog and wrote

Important as it is to gauge the extent to which the Negro group experience has ripened and flowered artistically, it is even more important to realize how proper and inevitable it is that this work be viewed and accepted as an integral and representative segment of our native American art. Indeed it runs the gamut of practically every well-known variety of modern art approach and style . . . other overtones suggest, however, common emotional factors of racial life and experience. . . . Further, the social message of the younger Negro artist is particularly noticeable and noteworthy. . . .[2]

Black artists were not always content to leave the exhibition of their works to others. In 1963 a group of New York artists banded together just before the historic march on Washington and formed a group called *Spiral.* Hale Woodruff, in answering the question of why the group was formed, answered that,

we as Negroes could not fail to be touched by the outrage of segregation or fail to relate to the self-reliance, hope and courage of those persons who were marching in the interest of man's dignity.[3]

1. Gwendolyn Bennett, *Exhibition of Works by Prominent Negro Artists.* (Harlem Community Art Center, 290 Lennox Ave., New York City. Federal Art Project, April 24-May 15 1939.)
2. Alaine Locke, "Up Till Now," in *The Negro Artist Comes of Age: A National Survey of Contemporary American Artists.* (Albany Institute of History and Art, January 3rd through February 11th, 1945.)
3. Introduction to Spiral exhibition catalog of May 15 to June 5, 1963. (147 Christopher Street, New York City 10014.)

Figure 2.1 Hale Woodruff. *Playground.* 1972. Oil, 40 x 44 inches. Reproduced by courtesy of Hale Woodruff.

Other members of Spiral included Charles Alston, Romare Bearden, Emma Amos, Calvin Douglass, Perry Ferguson, Alvin Hollingsworth, Reginald Gammon, Felrath Hines, Norman Lewis, Richard Mayhew, William Majors, Earl Miller, Merton Simpson, and James Yeargans.

In 1966 the California Arts Commission sponsored an exhibit, The Negro in American Art, which began at UCLA and traveled to other University of California campuses. James Porter's essay for the catalog traced the development of the Black artist in the United States and presented a fine critical analysis of this development. The following year Romare Bearden and Carroll Greene organized the New York City University exhibit, The Evolution of Afro-American Artists: 1800-1950 and Howard University produced Ten Afro-American Artists of the Nineteenth Century in celebration of the centennial of Howard University.

One of the most exciting exhibits of works by Black artists and works influenced by African arts was formed by students of Jehanne Teilhet of the University of California at San Diego and exhibited at the La Jolla Museum of Art in 1970. The amazing thing about this exhibit is that there were actually three exhibits in one: works by Black artists from colonial times to the present, traditional African art representing a number of styles, and works by

European artists strongly influenced by African art. Picasso's famous *Demoiselles d'Avignon* was loaned by the Museum of Modern Art as were other works influenced by African art by Matisse, Modigliani, Schmidt-Rotluff, Pechstein, Kirchner, Ernst, Lipchitz, and Moore. This exhibit, titled Dimensions of Black, was conceived and developed by Miss Teilhet and her students who wrote a major part of the catalog. In the catalog's introduction Henry Seldis wrote,

Neither pious promises nor militant confrontations, neither myths of white supremacy nor assertions of black separatism can touch the fervently affirmative reality of "Dimensions of Black."

The very making of this unique exhibition must serve as a primary example for dynamic and viable approaches to Afro-American studies on our campuses. . . .

Most revolutionary artists of any age ignored the standard biases of established society. The lot of the Bohemian artists of Paris in the teens and twenties of this century was not better than that of their black counterparts. Their commitments to individual freedom were and still are paralleled by the demands for freedom and equality voiced by all politically and ethnically oppressed.[4]

The exhibit catalog has provided opportunity for scholars and critics to express ideas and attitudes of a signal nature, different from the timelessness of books and the immediacy of periodicals. The development of ethnic studies departments has sparked numerous exhibits, such as the Herbert F. Johnson Museum of Art and the African Studies and Research Center of Cornell University. These in turn have inspired business, industry, and social organizations to initiate exhibits as those of the Illinois Bell Telephone exhibit of Black American Artists 71 and 17 Artists: Hispano, Mexican American, Chicano in 1976, The Afro-American Artist by the Delta Sigma Theta Sorority of Winston-Salem, North Carolina, and the National Links, Inc., in Cincinnati, Ohio. The nationwide Black protest movement has contributed to an increasing number of exhibits devoted to works by Black artists.

Whereas the above-mentioned exhibits were national in scope, there have been many more regional and local exhibits of works of these artists. In the main, these have not been as selective, but they have given a wider exposure to artists of the community. In 1968 Art West Association North [AWAN] produced New Perspectives in Black Art, which introduced artists of northern California, and the same year the Studio Museum was established in Harlem where instruction in art as well as exhibitions were held.

During the same year I produced an exhibit for Johnson C. Smith University, Charlotte, North Carolina, composed mainly of Black artists who had some ties with North Carolina. This was both regional and national in scope since most of the artists represented no longer lived in North Carolina. One objective of the exhibit was to present works of artists who might have contributed their creative talents to this community had they been encouraged to do so. This exhibit, titled Encounters, was the University's contribution to the bicentennial celebration of Charlotte and Mecklenburg County, North Carolina. Some of the artists were Charles Alston, Romare Bearden, John Biggers, Selma Burke, James Diggs, Walker Foster, Ethel Guest, Ernest Crichlow, Jacob Lawrence, Esther Hill, Henry O. Tanner, and George Love, all of whom had lived or worked in North Carolina. Robert Gwathmey, who uses the Negro as a subject, was the only non-Black artist in the exhibit. Other artists included had either influenced those from North Carolina or had been influenced by them.

In 1969 the Harlem Cultural Council and the School of Art and the Urban Center of Columbia University presented an exhibit, New Black Artists, at the Brooklyn Museum. Some of the artists, such as Joseph Overstreet, have since become nationally known.

The National Center of Afro-American Artists, a part of the Elma Lewis School of Fine Arts in the Boston suburb of Dorchester, has sparked a number of exhibits featuring Black artists. One, titled 5, showed the works of Romare Bearden, Jacob Lawrence, Horace Pippin, Charles White, and Hale Woodruff. Another, Lamp Black, produced in conjunction with the Museum of Fine Arts and the School of the Museum of Fine Arts in Boston showed the works of seventy artists. Among those included

4. Henry Seldis, "Introduction" to Dimensions of Black Catalog. Jehanne Teilhet, ed. (La Jolla: La Jolla Museum of Art, 1970).

Figure 2.2 Pablo Picasso. *Les Demoiselles d'Avignon.*
1907. Oil on canvas, 8 feet x 7 feet, 8 inches. Collection of
The Museum of Modern Art, New York. Acquired through
the Lillie P. Bliss Bequest.

Figure 2.3 John Biggers. *Family #1*. Conté crayon. Reproduced by courtesy of John Biggers.

Figure 2.4 John Biggers. *Family #2*. Conté crayon. Reproduced by courtesy of John Biggers.

were Calvin Burnett, Dana Chandler, Lois M. Jones, Gary Rickson, Al Smith, and John Wilson of Boston, and Benny Andrews, Malcom Bailey, Robert Blackburn, Emma Amos, Betty Blayton, Cliff Joseph, Eldzier Cortor, Ernest Crichlow, Emilo Cruz, Felrath Hines, Alvin Hollingsworth, Zell Ingram, Tom Lloyd, Richard Mayhew, Barbara Chase Riboud, Raymond Saunders, Vincent Smith, and Alma Thomas of New York. Catalog notes for the exhibit 5 were by Carroll Greene and the Lamp Black exhibit of Afro-American Artists, New York and Boston were by Edmund B. Gaither.

On the west coast, Mills College of Oakland, California, showed the works of nineteen Black craftsmen in 1970. This exhibit was organized by E. J. Montgomery and introduced weavers, silversmiths, potters, and jewelers under the title **California Black Craftsmen**. Among the nineteen included were Dale Davis, Manuel Gomez, Bob Jefferson, Evangeline Montgomery, and John Outterbridge.

Another source of information began in 1971 when the University of South Alabama developed a collection of slides by Black artists for sale to the public. In 1973 this collection was expanded to include works by Mexican-American and American Indian artists. In the same year the National Endowment for the Arts Expansion Program financed a research project, headed by Irene Sawyer at the University of California, Berkeley, to develop an archive on Afro-American art and artists.

Figure 2.5 Lois Mailou Jones. *Soap Vendors—Haiti.* Watercolor. Reproduced by courtesy of Lois Mailou Jones.

Figure 2.6 Ernie Crichlow. Untitled. Oil. Reproduced by courtesy of Ernie Crichlow.

Figure 2.7 Dan Concholar. Untitled. Acrylic on canvas. Reproduced by courtesy of Brockman Gallery Productions, Inc.

Figure 2.8 Eugenio Quesada. *Sonado*. Reproduced by courtesy of Eugenio Quesada.

In spite of the dramatic increase in the number of exhibits and publications devoted to works of artists who are Black, little attention has been given to them in texts used in school art curricula with a few exceptions. More attention or recognition seems to have been given in the 1940s than in the 1970s. Ralph Pearson's *The New Art Education,* published in 1941, included several works by Hale Woodruff and two of his students, Albert Wells and Robert Neal. These were not included as "ethnic" examples but as examples of design. Viktor Lowenfeld included works by John Biggers and Samella Sanders in *Creative and Mental Growth,* published in 1947, as examples of mural painting. These illustrations have been omitted in editions published since Lowenfeld's death. Neither Pearson nor Lowenfeld identified the artists as Negro, but their works were used as examples of design or mural painting. This underlies a contention of many ethnic artists, that their works should be included for the same reasons as those of other artists. Such inclusion provides double benefit for the art teacher as they serve as models for youth to emulate. On the other hand, their exclusion serves to alienate members of the ethnic communities, particularly the youth.

It was the Black community that first erupted against the inequities faced educationally, economically, and socially. The youth no longer sought to lose themselves in the major American scene since they saw this was impossible. Instead, their push was for a greater sense of self, of self-identity, and a search for cultural heritage. Campus after campus faced demands for Black studies and on some there were demands for separate dormitories and even soul food on the menu. These young people rejected three hundred years of attempts at integration with slogans indicating pride of heritage; "Black power," and "Black is beautiful."

The Spanish-Speaking Ethnics; Chicano/Mexican-American/Puerto Rican/Cuban/South American Artists

The effect of the movement of Black youth was not lost on other minorities, and rumblings began to be heard from the Spanish-speaking communities, which, even more than the Afro-Americans, had been misled into believing that they had no problems in ascending the "ladder of the American dream." This

Figure 2.9 Eugenio Quesada. *Nina.* Reproduced by courtesy of Eugenio Quesada.

group, largely of Mexican heritage in the West and Puerto Rican in the East, had only to lose their accents, forget their culture, and join the mainstream of American society in order to "make it." A few made it and vanished into the mainstream. The fact that the census identifies the group as White rather than non-White made it easier to develop a feeling of superiority to the non-White. In the Southwest, before the 1954 Supreme Court decision, and for some time afterwards, the Mexican-American child was as rigidly segregated in schools as the Black child. The larger the community was, the tighter the segregation. The small communities could not afford separate schools. In small mining towns of the West, often the majority of the population was Mexican-American, and seldom were there any Blacks. The affluent minority of Whites sent their children to boarding schools, leaving the largest population in the schools to be of Mexican descent. On the other hand, teachers were likely to be Anglo, unable to

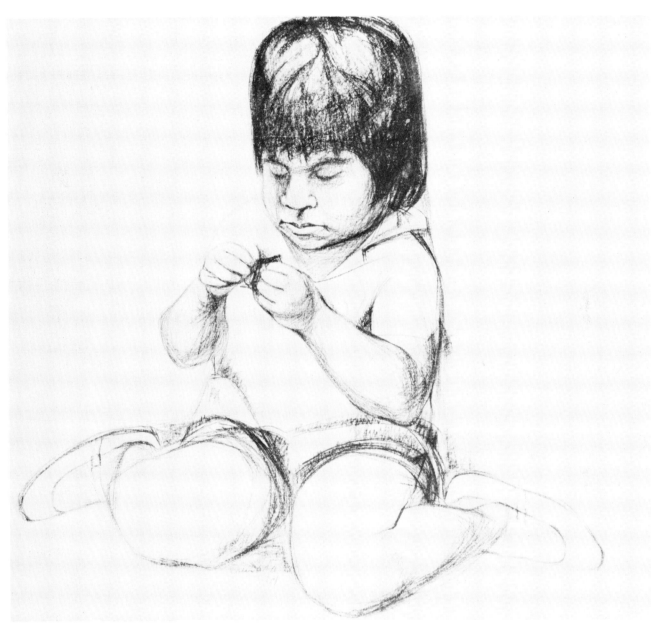

Figure 2.10 Eugenio Quesada. *Nina Traviesta*. Reproduced by courtesy of Eugenio Quesada.

speak Spanish, and with little understanding of the cultural background of these children. As a result, the identity crisis among Mexican-Americans was likely to be as great as that of Black children. This search for identity is reflected in name identification: Spanish-American, Mexican-American, and Chicano. The older, more conservative generation seems to prefer Spanish-American; the middle generation chose Mexican-American, and the militant youth prefer "Chicano." A letter to the editor of the *Arizona*

Republic on July 21, 1974 titled "Chicano not Unsuitable Name" is written in protest to another writer who rejected the name "Chicano." The writer sees no reason ". . . to romanticize our beginnings."

When we were growing up in pre-World War II Arizona, we were generally referred to as DAMNED DIRTY MEXICANS; we dutifully trudged off across town to our segregated school, took our place in the section of the movie theatre

Figure 2.11 David Nunez. Untitled. Pencil. Reproduced by courtesy of David Nunez.

Figure 2.12 David Nunez. Untitled. Pencil. Reproduced by courtesy of David Nunez.

that was set aside for the likes of us—we stayed properly outside of the fenced-in public park and CERTAINLY out of the public swimming pool. We were denied the right to own property in restricted neighborhoods, and I, for one, was denied a hair cut, . . . while wearing the uniform of the U. S. Army Air Corps.

We were not immigrants. Our family traces its roots to beyond United States possession of these parts. Our lands were confiscated, and we ourselves became the booty of the "Mexican War." We are a captive people. Still.

Mexico abandoned us. We have no ties or claims there. How, then, are we Mexican?

The United States denied us full citizenship, and its people, the unhyphenated Americans, treated us for the most part a goodly amount lower than human. Where are we then Americans?

We not only accepted this shabby treatment, we uttered not one word in protest.

Call yourself a Mexican-American if you want to, Maria, I find more comfort with a title that needs no apologies nor hyphenations. The Chicano, after all, is a person of Mexican descent, who, living in the United States experienced neither a true Mexican nor a true American life.[5]

The gravity of this problem did not fully strike me until 1965 when I was asked to produce an exhibit for the first Conference on Poverty in the Southwest. Robert B. Choate organized the conference and Vice-President Humphrey was the major speaker. The job was to organize an exhibit of works representing successful artists who had come from a

5. Pedro E. Guerrero, "Chicano not Unsuitable Name," Letter to the Editor, *Arizona Republic* (Phoenix), 21 July 1974.

Figure 2.13 Luis Baiz. *Evil Lurks Within Our World.*
Pencil. Reproduced by courtesy of Luis Baiz.

background of poverty. This was an opportunity to
include and identify artists of a variety of ethnic
backgrounds, since minority people are most often at
the lower end of the economic ladder.

There was no problem getting representation from
the White, Black, and Red artists of the southwestern
states of California, Nevada, Utah, Colorado, Arizona,
New Mexico, and Texas. I was amazed at the difficulty in identifying and securing works by artists
who were citizens of the United States but of Mexican
heritage, especially since they comprised the largest
minority population in the southwest and since
one of the major art movements of the continent was
led by Mexican artists, such as Rivera, Orozco,
Tamayo, Siqueros, and a number of others. It grad-

ually became clear that the identity crisis might be a
crucial factor in the production of creative expression.
Our search was not fruitless, and we did find representation from this segment of the community, but
it was difficult. This experience taught me, a high
school teacher, the importance of including works by
Mexican artists in class discussions, to indicate to
students the contributions to world art by artists of
the Mexican ethnic heritage on both sides of the
border.

Literature dealing with the Mexican-American or
Chicano artist is even more difficult to find than
that on the Black artist. There is a vast store
of material on the arts of Mexico, but the first published article that I found on the contemporary

15

Figure 2.14 Gilbert Atencio. *Basket Dance*. Tempera. From the collection of the Heard Museum, Phoenix, Arizona.

Mexican-American artist was by Dr. Jacinto Quirarte in the second quarter, 1970 issue of *Humble Way*. This article was developed into a book of the same name, published by the University of Texas Press.

In his book Dr. Quirarte traces the Mexican-American artists from the beginning of the century through 1946. He divides this time block into four decades and presents artists important in each decade. The first decade, 1901-1912, covers the works of Antonio Garcia, Chelo Amezuca, Octavio Medellin, Margaret Chávez, and Porfirio Salinas. His second time division is 1915-1923, which includes Edward Chavez, Michael Ponce de Leon, Ruben Gonzales, Pedro Cervantez, and Joel Tito Ramirez. For the third decade he uses the period 1926-1934, which includes Peter Rodriguez, Eugenio Quesada, Melesio Casas, Emilo Aguirre, Manuel Neri, Louis Gutierrez, Ernesto

Palomino, and Ralph Ortiz. The fourth includes Eduardo Carillo, Ray Chavez, Joseph Chavez, Michael Lopez, and Luis Jiminez in the first part, and Amado Pena, Glynn Gomez, Rudy Trevino, and Alex Sanchez in the second part of that period. Quirarte gives a brief introduction to each artist telling something of the life and the works of each artist. The final chapters are devoted to a discussion of the name problem, Mexican-American or Chicano.

The number of Mexican-American/Chicano artists has steadily grown since the beginning of the century. Quirarte presents five for each of the first two decades, eight for the third, and nine for the fourth. There are certainly many more than this number that have gone unrecognized. I organized an exhibit titled Five Chicano Artists in 1971 and only one of those listed by Dr. Quirarte, Eugenio Quesada, was included. The other four were Luis Baiz, Fernando Navarro, David Nuñez, and Saul Solache. Solache, from California, was the only one not from Arizona.

Teachers and students would profit by seeking out artists of Chicano or Spanish heritage in the community for interviews and exhibits, since available written material is scarce.

The Native American Indian Artists

Written material concerning the arts of the American Indian is voluminous. The extensive writing of Franz Boas covering the art and ethnology of many Indians and the volumes of Edward Curtis did much to lay the groundwork for understanding the life and art of the American Indian. The Indian was a subject of curiosity to the invading settlers, hunters, cowboys, and farmers. Collectors of Indian "curios," not considered as art in early years and still not by some "art lovers," began soon after the arrival of the European on American shores. Many of these collections are now found in major museums, and they have provided the source material for exhibits and publications. The Heye Foundation's Museum of the American Indian has one of the most extensive collections. The Field Museum, the Fred Harvey collection and the Denver Museum are but three with excellent collections of Indian art. A number of

Figure 2.15 Harrison Begay. *Deer Hunt*. Tempera. From the collection of the Heard Museum, Phoenix, Arizona.

Figure 2.16 Helen Codero. *Manger Scene*. Ceramic. From the collection of the Heard Museum, Phoenix, Arizona.

Figure 2.17 Harrison Begay. Untitled. From the collection of the Heard Museum, Phoenix, Arizona.

Figure 2.18 Oscar Howe. *Sun Dance*. From the collection of the Heard Museum, Phoenix, Arizona.

museums, such as the Heard Museum of Primitive Art and Anthropology in Phoenix, are devoted mainly to collecting, displaying, and promoting works by Indian artists.

Extensive ethnographic study of the Indian began in the nineteenth century, and much of it was reported by the Bureau of Ethnology. The works of Boas and Curtis have already been mentioned, and W. H. Dahl wrote about masks in 1884. Most studies were more concerned with ethnography than aesthetics, but one of the early publications to emphasize aesthetics was by Fredrick Douglas and Rene D'Harnoncourt, *Indian Art of the United States* published in 1941. In 1940, the Denver Museum had already produced a study of Indian masks by Douglas. R. T. Davis' *Native Arts of the Pacific Northwest* was published in 1949, and R. Bruce Inverarity's *Art of the Northwest Coast* was published in 1950.

Eckert von Sydow included American Indian art in his *Die Kunst, der Naturvölker und der Vorzeit* in

1923. Paul Wingert concentrated on *American Indian Sculpture* in 1949. Fredrick Dockstader's *Indian Art in America* in 1960 and Norman Feder's *American Indian Art* in 1965 are handsome publications, giving broad coverage to the art of the American Indian. It is interesting that none of the above authors, as far as I am aware, were Indians themselves. Neither was Frank Waters, who, in *Masked Gods,* gives an interesting view of the ceremonies of the Navajo and Pueblo people. In the course of this writing, Waters has provided much information about the different peoples, who populated the Western Hemisphere before the coming of Columbus. The book was written from the point of a journalist who had an intimate knowledge of the Indians as opposed to the viewpoint of an ethnologist, an aesthetician, or perhaps an Indian.

Most works illustrated in these writings are identified by tribe or region, particularly those that are more traditional, for individual artists were either un-

Figure 2.19 David Chethlahe Paladin. *Serpent Altar.*
Acrylic on canvas, 16 x 12 inches. Reproduced by courtesy of David Chethlahe Paladin.

Figure 2.20 Fred Kabotie. *Kachinas*. From the collection of the Heard Museum, Phoenix, Arizona.

known or ignored in early books and articles. More recent texts such as Feder's *American Indian Art,* Dorothy Dunn's *American Indian Painting,* and J. J. Brody's *Indian Painters and White Patrons,* introduce a number of contemporary artists: Blackbear Bosin, Tony Agilar, J. J. Garcia, Allan Houser, Oscar Howe, Harrison Begay, Veronica Cruz, Fred Kabotie, Patrick Hinds, Maria Martinez, Fritz Scholder, and R. C. Gorman. Emphasis on Indian Art has moved from ethnographic to aesthetic and, as a result, exhibit catalogs have introduced a number of artists. Tony Begay, Joan Hill, David Chethlahe Paladin, Mike Romero, Clifford Beck, Charles Loloma, Douglas Crowder, Dick West, and Franklin Fireshaker are some of those whose works are increasingly seen.

In spite of the attention paid to the Indians and the voluminous material written about them and their

work, the Indian artists have remained as invisible in the general art texts for classroom use as the Afro-Americans and the Mexican-Americans. The younger generation of Indians, like the Mexican-Americans who prefer to be known as Chicano and the Afro-Americans who prefer to be called Black, have been demanding self-respect and have been building a strong self-image. Indian arts have played a dominant role in developing this self-image, as they have in Indian culture. Many continue to work within a traditional style, but quite a few are welding traditional and new to create unique styles of their own. Lloyd New, Director of the Institute of American Indian Art in Santa Fe, has been an innovator of this movement. Fred Kabotie and Allan Houser represent the more traditional artists, David Chethlahe Paladin and Oscar Howe, the transitional in-between

Figure 2.21 Patrick Swazo Hinds. *Chant to the Corn Maiden*. Oil. From the collection of the Heard Museum, Phoenix, Arizona.

group, and Fritz Scholder and R. C. Gorman represent the new perspective. The Philbrook Art Center of Tulsa, the Scottsdale National Indian Arts Exhibition, the Oklahoma Art Center, and the Heard Museum's National Indian Art Exhibition, are but four of the annual exhibits featuring works of traditional and contemporary Indian art.

Summary

This is by no means an exhaustive survey of source materials available about the Black, Brown, and Red artists. It is sufficient to open the door of curiosity and provide background information for students and teachers who wish greater understanding of artists from these backgrounds. Such information should be valuable for those who seek artist models for youth from these ethnic backgrounds.

3 Ethnic Understanding and Art Education

The understanding gained in producing the exhibit for the National Conference on Poverty in Tucson, Arizona was background material for the presentation made at the Pacific Art Association Conference in Portland. Even more important was my experience of teaching high school youth from a variety of cultural backgrounds, where I learned how important one's heritage could be in the process of getting involved in art activities. I have seen angry, belligerent, and frustrated students, who cared little about school and were ready to erupt at any moment into violence, become actively absorbed in producing art and undergo a change in attitude. I have seen apathetic students, for the same reason, get involved and come to life through art activities.[1] In most instances, however, more than just materials and art activities were involved to create the change in attitude. Most of these students were from minority ethnic cultures and from the bottom of the economic pile. Usually they discovered someone with whom they could relate and saw an example of someone like themselves who had succeeded. This factor of discovering a model seemed to be as important as learning to handle materials successfully.

The 1972 National Art Education Association Conference, Pacific Regional, was conceived and developed with the idea of exploring cultural heritages. The conference theme, "Celebrations of Peoples," and the Honolulu setting worked towards this common end. Each session of the conference explored the idea of cultural heritage, and the support of schools and museums of Honolulu was magnificent. For the introduction to the convention program I wrote the following.

This NAEA Pacific Regional CELEBRATION OF PEOPLES, "Celebrates" through exploring the arts and cultures of the Pacific Region for better understanding of Peoples through their arts. Some elements of understanding can be uncovered in the short span of time we are here.

The U.S.A. has long been considered a "Melting Pot" which shaped the lives of immigrants and their descendants into a homogenous mass. This has been true for only a small minority, for most have fiercely maintained much of their cultural heritage. Instead of a "melting pot," a "stew pot" or as Kaprow put it, "A Mulligan Stew," may be a more apt description of the relations of peoples, their cultures, and their arts, in this country. Each maintains most of its identity while contributing to the flavor of the whole. This mixture of flavors, textures, colors, shapes, and aromas include: the Native American Indians; Mexican-Americans, . . . African forms come via the southern states; other ingredients to heighten the flavor are from the Orient, and the islands of the Pacific. All are intertwined with song and dance. Add these to those of Western Europe, and one truly has a "Mulligan Stew," remarkably delicious when all ingredients are respected and admired for their differences and for what they add to the flavor. When parts are unknown, feared, or not respected, the taste is not so pleasing. . . .

Tensions between peoples of different cultures, life styles, value systems, aspirations, and expres-

1. Eugene Grigsby, "Art Education at Carver High School," in *Art Education Journal* 7 (May 1954).

sions have increased in recent years, and on occasion, have exploded violently. Youth in particular, seek greater humaneness through cultural identity, recognition and self-respect.

Hastily constructed Ethnic courses have sought to assuage feelings of youth seeking cultural roots. Many of these are "band-aids" on social ills. The arts, in many instances however, have provided a valid source of curriculum building for much needed cultural respect and self-image construction. Of all the activities of non-western peoples, historically, the arts have commanded the greatest respect. Perhaps, through these expressions, respect for the people creating the arts may be generated. They cannot, however serve only as escape valves, used mainly to lessen tensions, and they can never be a panacea for social ills. They can serve as guide posts to mark directions and floodlights to illumine the way. They can be a beginning to a sensitive understanding of Peoples.

It is one objective of this conference to begin the arduous task of turning on the floodlights to recognize the accomplishments of Peoples different from those of Western European cultures. There is no intent to downgrade the accomplishments of European culture but rather, to add to these by recognition of the contributions of other Peoples often omitted from texts, films, and other media. . . .

For the classroom teacher, who must relate to a variety of youth who come increasingly from the "Third World," this understanding is vital to the improvement of teaching particularly to teaching art. . . .[2]

The keynote speech of the conference was delivered by Dr. Marcus Foster, late superintendent of Oakland Public Schools, who was tragically assassinated a year later. Dr. Foster told the audience how important a role art activities played in changing the attitudes of students at a Philadelphia high school from angry, belligerent, and apathetic students with little self-respect into eager, cooperative, inventive students with strong self-images. Gratz High School was dubbed "Gratz is for rats" when Foster was assigned to the school over the heads and objections of several administrators in line for the job. The difficulty of the job he faced was compounded by opposition of the faculty, because he was the first Black principal and the staff was mostly White.

Figure 3.1 David Chethlahe Paladin. *Sacred Circle.* Sand painting, 12 x 24 inches. Reproduced by courtesy of David Chethlahe Paladin.

2. Eugene Grigsby, "Introduction," *Celebration of Peoples.* (Program of the NAEA Pacific Regional Conference, Honolulu, March 1972.)

Figure 3.2 David Chethlahe Paladin. *Cave Wall: Ancient Anasazi Figures*. Sand on panel, 30 x 48 inches. Reproduced by courtesy of David Chethlahe Paladin.

Eighteen students graduated at the end of his first year and few of these, if any, went on to college. At the end of the second year the dropout rate was cut in half, and 168 students graduated and 128 of these were accepted into college. The full story is told in his book, *Making Schools Work*, but not as much emphasis is given to the role the arts played in the book as he gave in his keynote address. He talked of the need for change in the attitudes of teachers and the need for models for youth. He wrote

Students will learn of the contributions of Negroes to art and music. . . . They will discover that culture is a tapestry made up of black threads, white threads, yellow threads, and other colors, all woven together. Our task will be to put the black threads back where they belong in the tapestry because when one leaves out the major contributions of any part of mankind, one distorts the entire pattern of culture.[3]

Later he added,

One can make a distinction of course, between acquiring these useful middle-class skills and accepting all the middle-class values. It makes great sense for a teacher to point out the advantages of being able to speak standard American English. Naturally the teacher will provide instruction in it. But this is very different from a teacher's disparaging the personal aesthetic values of a student who sees himself part of the non-middle-class culture. And if the teacher finds himself contemptuous of his student's manner of dress or choice of music, he has an obligation to himself and to his students to find work elsewhere, with children he can more easily relate to.[4]

3. Marcus Foster, *Making Schools Work*, p. 120. Copyright © 1971 by the Westminster Press. Used by permission of the publisher.

4. Ibid, p. 127.

Figure 3.3 Alan Houser. *The Wild Horses.* From the collection of the Heard Museum, Phoenix, Arizona.

Although the NAEA Honolulu Conference was stimulating, innovative, and rewarding in presenting the arts of a variety of cultures, it tended to raise as many questions as it answered. William Glaeser, writing in *Studies in Art Education,* the NAEA Journal of Issues and Research in Art Education, makes a scholarly critique of the conference, probing its meaning and possible consequences in both positive and negative aspects.

We as art educators must be extremely aware of the possible consequences of our actions. They are both positive and negative. The positive conse-

quences are fairly obvious. By our aesthetic and intellectual involvement and understanding in the arts and the diverse socio-cultural variables that influence and are influenced by the arts, significant contributions can be made to ourselves and to our students by broadening and deepening our concepts of the human and natural dimensions of the world in which we live. This can be seen as a very powerful contribution to the solution of many world problems.

An important question related to negative implications must not be ignored. To what extent will our attempts to understand and utilize different cultural points of view and in the development of

Figure 3.4 R. C. Gorman. Untitled. Lithograph. From the collection of the Heard Museum, Phoenix, Arizona.

our own world concepts destroy that which we are here to celebrate. . . .[5]

Glaeser's concern for possible positive or negative consequences on the future shape of the arts, education, and living, based on aesthetic and intellectual involvements, demands serious consideration. The sociocultural variables that influence and are influenced by the arts have been present throughout the history of the United States. Although these variables have existed, they have not been obvious, since they are so much a part of the fabric of the major culture. Economic, social, and political factors of sociocultural variables have done as much as, or more than, aesthetic ones to shape the direction, meaning,

and use of the arts. In the United States these factors have also served to close out forms and concepts alien to the majority culture. People of the minority ethnic cultures, major subjects of the three conferences mentioned above, tended to be unique, sometimes exotic, and usually different in skin color, hair texture, and language; furthermore, they would not melt or fade away. Works produced by these people and their ancestors were also different. Art teachers, mostly from the majority community, attending the Tucson, Portland, and Honolulu con-

5. William Glaeser, "Art Concepts of Reality, and the Consequences of The Celebrations of Peoples," *Studies in Art Education* 15, no. 1 (1973): 34-43.

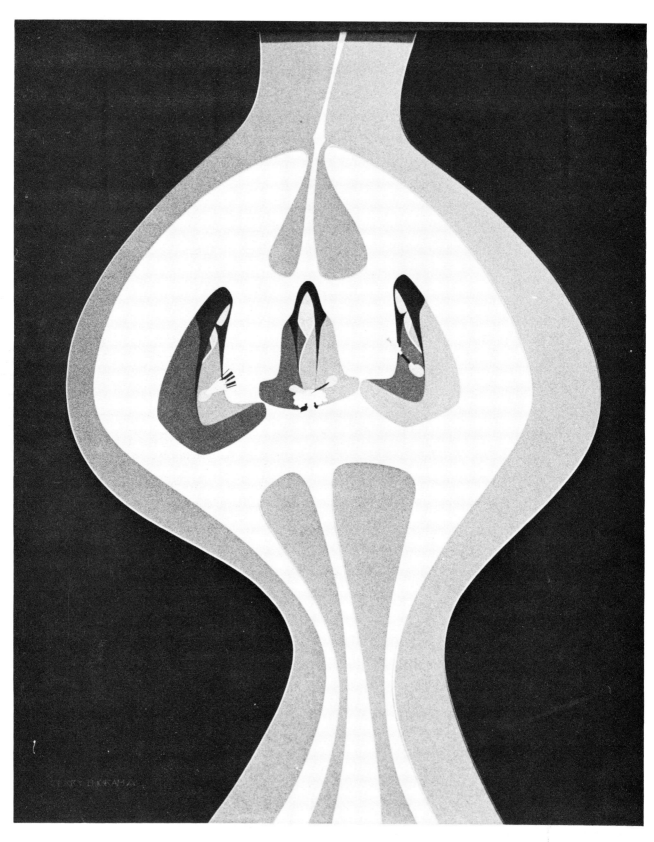

Figure 3.5 Jerry Ingram. *Native American*. From the
collection of the Heard Museum, Phoenix, Arizona.

Figure 3.6 J. D. Roybal. Untitled. From the collection of the Heard Museum, Phoenix, Arizona.

ferences sought to gain information about certain cultural components or sociocultural variables as reflected in the lives and the arts of people from the minority socioeconomic communities.

We now ask, what *is* the majority culture? Is it a monolith of peoples with similar expressions and feelings into which those of the minority group mentioned above refuse to fade or melt? Are there communities and cultures within this majority community with their own uniqueness, as different from one another as they are from the minority communities? If these differences exist, and there are reasons to believe they do, has there been significant exchange between these segments of the majority and minority communities? If the exchange between segments of the minority communities has resulted in positive or negative results for each and if there has been exchange between one or more of the majority communities with one or more of the minority communities, have there also been positive or negative results? If these exchanges have taken place and the positive or negative results noted, can the results be used for information and motivational purposes in the classroom?

What are the differences between the majority and minority communities that remain constant?

Who were the original inhabitants of the United States? Where did the immigrants originate? Have all vestiges of original culture that they brought from other lands been eliminated, or do some still exist among those of the majority culture?

Are the differenecs within the majority culture as great as those differences which separate the majority from the minority cultures?

Is the sum of the differences between the three large minority cultures as great as that between the different segments of the majority culture?

Are the differences within the groups as great as they are between groups?

Will the answers to these questions be of as great a value to art teachers in the search to become more effective, as technical information about styles, movements in art history, materials, techniques of handling materials, design, and theories of design equipment and other methodology?

Answers to these questions are the concern of the following chapters.

4 Need for Awareness of Cultural Differences: Models for Students

Foremost among objectives and desires of art teachers, as with most teachers, is to devise ways for more effective teaching. The high school art teacher is often faced with the task of teaching a variety of skills and subject matter to an increasingly varied student population. The effectiveness of teaching skills and subject matter depends, to a large degree, on how well the teacher understands and can communicate with the students. Prior to the 1954 Supreme Court decision that schools should desegregate "with all deliberate speed," teachers and students were more likely to be of similar social and/or economic backgrounds and hold values that were more alike than different. Segregated schools tended to insure a certain homogeneity of students and teachers, particularly in the southern and western states. Many northern and eastern states were likely to be equally segregated due to neighborhood segregation patterns, but often in poor Black, Brown, and Red neighborhoods many teachers were White and middle class.

Since 1954 the racial population of schools has been increasingly mixed, breaking down the previous homogeneity between students and teachers. One result of this change has been an increasing difficulty of teachers and students to understand and communicate with one another, a condition that has made the teaching of skills and subject matter more difficult. The variety of life-styles, cultural value sets, and a myriad of minor differences form undercurrents of conflict, which make teaching difficult for those who concentrate mainly on developing skills and presenting subject matter without seriously taking into consideration different value systems, life-styles, and other social differences that exist between teacher and student.

The change in the physical appearances of youth in the classrooms, from being either Black or White to that of a mixture of both, has created a need to know more about the youth who populate these classrooms—who they are, where they come from, what they value, what they like and dislike—and the need to know more about their cultural and ethnic heritage. In the search to learn something about the different looking and sometimes different acting, speaking, walking, working, and playing student, there is a dawning realization that even the ones who appear to be similar may also be quite different from one another. Many who appear to be racially similar may be quite different ethnically. It becomes evident that there exists no monolithic Black, White, Red, Brown, or Yellow peoples who can be expected to respond in like manner to the same set of stimuli.

An editorial in the January 1970 issue of *Music Educator's Journal*, titled "Urban Culture, Awareness May Save Our Skins," presents the problems many teachers face.

The face of America's cities is pockmarked. Mass exodus has left festering inner cities—domiciles of the destitute victims of disease, hunger, crime, drugs, broken families, and hopelessness. Poverty, segregation, and bankruptcy blight the people and thwart the work of every institution. The poor—be they white, black, Mexican-American, or Puerto Rican—bring their environment with them

Figure 4.1   Edward Judie. *Head #2.* Mesquite wood. Reproduced by courtesy of the author.

Figure 4.2   Edward Judie. *Head.* Ironwood. Reproduced by courtesy of the author.

into the schools. Society's sickness touches every subject in the curriculum, including music. The strain on every subject has been severe. It is breaking the backbone of many city music programs. Experienced music teachers are leaving the profession or fleeing to the safety of the suburbs. The status of music in the cities is crumbling under an avalanche of ferment, frustration, and failure.

So serious and so widespread are the problems, that the time has come for music educators to reassess their purposes and their programs. In the ghetto, music teachers find that every ideal they were taught to adhere to seems to be open to attack or, at least, seriously questioned. Worst of all, the so-called "tried and true" approaches fail to work. Music teachers in the ghetto soon discover an enormous gap. Not a generation gap, but a much more confusing and devastating one—a gap between their middle class values and the particular values held by their students. There is often a vast difference between the teacher's and the student's cultures. . . . He isn't "turned on" by cowboy

songs. He won't easily enthuse [sic] over studying stringed instruments. He doesn't want our Lincoln Centers. He isn't interested in classical music; in fact, he'll tell you with complete certainty how dull it sounds compared to James Brown or Aretha Franklin. The old image, the old ways, and the old music education curriculum are developing cracks. They don't work in the ghetto. Not only that, there is evidence that what happens on the front lines is becoming an epidemic that is certain to spread to the suburbs and beyond.[1]

Conditions cited in this editorial are not limited to music teachers, since the same might be said of the art teacher as well as of those of other subject matter areas. For some teachers this realization of cultural differences tends to make teaching difficult, whereas for others it makes teaching exciting. For the former there is a slowdown in the imparting of subject matter and the development of skills because the students don't understand as well as the others, are dumb or lazy, or can't think, won't pay attention, have poor attendance, and numerous other reasons. For the latter teachers, this great variety of youth offers new and different opportunities, and each student is a challenge to be met in a new and exciting way.

The latter group of teachers, who dig into backgrounds of individuals and communities, discover many ways of reaching and teaching students who are culturally, ethnically, and/or racially different from themselves. There are many examples of teachers who succeeded in reaching students different from themselves. Sylvia Ashton-Warner tells in her books *Spinster* and *Teacher* how she, an English woman, was able to teach young Maori children in New Zealand through understanding and respect of their culture in spite of cultural differences and stifling bureaucratic British rules. E. R. Braithwaite describes in *To Sir With Love*, his success as a Black teacher from Georgetown, Guiana, in an English school and the problems he had to overcome. The example given by Marcus Foster is but one of many that might be of particular interest to art teachers.

It is increasingly difficult for teachers to "escape" to schools where they find students of a homogenous background, with whom they can more easily relate. It behooves teachers and those planning to teach to understand something of the cultural and ethnic differences of students they are likely to encounter in any of the schools of the United States. Few examples as dramatic as those related by Foster have been published, but they exist, particularly in the large urban centers. Many innovative experiments have been carried out during the 1960s and early 1970s, which have been reported in conferences and seminars.

The Seminar on Elementary and Secondary Art Education convened by Howard Conant at New York University; the conference on *The Role of the Arts in Meeting the Social and Educational Needs of the Disadvantaged,* initiated by Hanna T. Rose and held at the Brooklyn Museum; *The Arts and the Black Revolution,* reported in *Arts in Society,* Summer/Fall 1968; *CONFABA* a *Conference on the Functional Aspects of Black Art,* organized by Jeff Donaldson at Northwestern University, 1970; and The Black Academy of Arts and Letters conference, *To Assess the State of Black Arts and Letters in the United States,* held in 1972 in Chicago, have pointed to directions of communication. Important sessions of the National Art Education Association's national, regional, and mini-conferences have been devoted to improving the quality of teaching art through improved communication with people of different cultural and ethnic backgrounds. This is also a major aim of the International Society of Education Through Art.

Although many fine examples of successful teaching have been cited at these conferences and seminars, they were usually isolated and confined to a single classroom, or else they were carried on outside the regular school. Research studies relating to teaching the culturally different have doubled in recent years, but these have been usually conducted in short periods of time and in clinically isolated situations. Few examples of the type cited by Foster that require years of development, dedicated teachers and administrators, and community involvement are to be found. They exist, I am sure, but

Figure 4.3 Jacob Lawrence. *Builders*. Gouache. Reproduced by the courtesy of Jacob Lawrence and from the collection of the Vatican Museum, Rome.

1. Charles B. Fowler, ed., "Urban Culture, Awareness May Save Our Skins," *Music Educators Journal* 56, no. 5 (January, 1970): 37. Copyright 1970 by Music Educators National Conference. Reprinted by permission of *Music Educators Journal.*

Figure 4.4 Alberoi Brazile (Haiti). *Leaving Church.* 1967. Oil on masonite, 30 x 24 inches. Reproduced by the courtesy of Mr. and Mrs. John H. Hewitt.

seldom are they publicized because the participants
have little time or interest in writing about the
results, and often they are too close to the picture to
see what has happened in relation to other schools. I
have personally witnessed two such situations, but
only in retrospect realize the significance of either.
One was as a high school student in North Carolina,
where my father was principal during the Depression
years of the early 1930s. Many symptoms of today's
ghetto schools were quite apparent: absenteeism, al-
coholism, high dropout rate, insolence, disrespect
for teachers, constant fights, students with knives and
guns, and little concern for academic excellence.
Over a period of nearly thirty years the attitudes and
conditions changed drastically, and when the school
was closed, due to integration, the alumni of the
school was highly respected and formed the core of a
prominent community of professionals. Years later
as a faculty member of a school quite similar to the
one described by Marcus Foster, although much
smaller and in a western city, I witnessed a principal
and educator, W. A. Robinson, advocate and put
into practice in the years following World War II
policies now being advocated in leading educational
journals. Few of us as teachers would have predicted
even in our wildest dreams, the professional success
that has been achieved by some of the students who
came to this school, but Robinson had confidence
in their potential and pushed faculty, staff, and community to recognize these potentials and to encourage
students to live up to them. This was accomplished
by hard work; weekly faculty meetings, many lasting
a long time; involvement of students and parents
in faculty meetings and other consultations; and constant probing into problems of learning faced by
parents, students, and faculty with a minimum of
violation of personal values. Of course, we as the
faculty resisted many of these ideas and methods,
but the results paid off. Before it closed, both students
and faculty were highly regarded. Many of its grad-
uates now hold important positions in different parts
of the country. Neither of these schools exist today
as they have been absorbed in the path of "integration," but the lesson they taught should not be

Figure 4.5   Luener Lazard (Haiti). *Remembrance of
Port-au-Prince*. Oil on canvas. Reproduced by courtesy
of Mr. and Mrs. John H. Hewitt.

forgotten—that youth from the lowest common denominator of society have a potential of success in the major community. Surely other similar examples exist throughout the country but have not been publicized. Probably every art teacher has seen an individual student tune in and turn on to some phase of art, especially when that student was able to relate to and be inspired by someone or something from his or her own heritage. This, I believe, is part of the secret of the two examples cited. Both were predominantly Black schools, and the teachers were able to cite examples of successful people in different professions who had come from backgrounds similar to their students. An example of what I mean was reported in an article published in the May 1954 issue of *Art Education*. A student, who was a potential dropout and somewhat of a troublemaker, "who carved on desks and fellow students," turned on to sculpture. Some twenty years later he returned home for a visit and made a point of paying his former high school art teacher a visit to tell how important his art classes and interest in sculpture had been in his deciding to enlist in the army. Subsequent success in the army as a noncommissioned officer in food services and a specialist in "ice sculpture" had been due to early interest in sculpture. (See figures 4.1 and 4.2.)

Need for Representative Models from Diverse Populations

A major factor present in these schools, which this writer believes has not been given the significance it deserves, is the use of "models" to whom students can relate and emulate. Students attending majority schools, predominantly Caucasian, are constantly presented models with whom they can identify geographically and ethnically. Most art classes, whether studio or art history, will touch upon European art and artists; English, French, German, Spanish, and so forth, whose backgrounds will be similar to many members of the class. References to African or American Indian art are usually made in the context of "primitive, exotic, or strange" in the sense that these are interesting but not works to be used as models to emulate. Few historical or contemporary examples of American artists of African or American Indian background are included in the average class, because few are readily available in general art texts.

Figure 4.6 Elton Fax. *In the Marketplace.* Conté crayon. Reproduced by courtesy of Elton Fax.

Students attending schools that were predominantly Black, Brown, or Red were taught by teachers of similar ethnic heritage or by teachers sensitive to the needs of these students. They always included the basic art history background, but they also included works by artists whose ethnic and cultural backgrounds were similar to those of the students of the class. This was particularly true in southern schools before the 1954 Supreme Court decision because many of the art teachers received their training in predominantly Black universities and colleges where work by Black artists were well known. Moreover, many of these teachers were themselves likely to be practicing artists. Henry O. Tanner, Hale Woodruff, Aaron Douglas, Meta Warrick Fuller, Charles White, and Augusta Savage are some of the names as common to these students as Rembrandt, da Vinci, Michelangelo,

Matisse, and Picasso. Students at Carver High School in Phoenix were fascinated to learn that the chemist, George Washington Carver, for whom the school had been named, had once considered becoming an artist. Twenty-seven of his oil paintings hang in the Iowa Carver Art Collection and four of his paintings were selected for the World's Columbian Exposition held in Chicago in 1893 to celebrate the four hundredth anniversary of Columbus's discovery of America. One received honorable mention. Carver was then twenty-nine and a senior at Iowa State College. Although Carver went on to make many discoveries, creating over three hundred products from the peanut and one hundred eighteen from the sweet potato, which added greatly to the economy of the country, his humanitarian interests in art and music seem to have been virtually forgotten.

Few students from the minority community, as well as their White counterparts, have been aware of African arts or their impact on arts of other countries. For the most part, Black, Brown, Red, and Yellow, as well as White, students fall prey to the propaganda about Africa, dating back to the fifteenth century when such propaganda was used to gain support for the slave trade. The residue of these arguments continue to leave the imprint of inferiority on those of African heritage and is used as a means of justifying their exploitation.

Historically, the majority and minority peoples of the United States have been divided into Black, Red, and White. Many of the Indians, original inhabitants and commonly called "Red" people, were marched off to the West and confined to reservations. The numerically smaller Orientals of Chinese, Japanese, and other Eastern ancestry, are found mainly on the West coast. Subsequent census figures will identify these numbers. In the Southwest, those of Mexican ancestry were comfortable in their official classification by the census as White, although they were segregated in schools and housing. Among themselves they continued to maintain a strong ethnic identification.

The Black population of the United States reached its greatest percentage in 1820 when it was 19% of the total population, and the lowest point in 1920, one hundred years later, when it dropped to 9.9%. Since that time there has been a gradual rise in the percentage of the Black population and it now stands at roughly 11%. These percentages reveal the demand for Black workers needed to bolster the economy at the height of the slave trade. The lowest figure reveals, in part, the attempts of anti-Black forces to drive Blacks out of the country.

There is much evidence that a large minority community will be a part of the national picture for many years to come. The September 6, 1974 issue of the *Christian Science Monitor* predicted that by the year 2000 the Spanish surname population will outnumber the Black. Illegal immigrants from Mexico, and Central and South America will add to this swell in population. Even though they have Spanish surnames and speak a brand of Spanish, they will present problems of understanding and motivation for the classroom teacher due to the strong differences between them. There is also evidence that the Oriental population is rising. These include not only Chinese and Japanese, but Korean, Vietnamese, Cambodians, and other Far Eastern countries. They, too, will add to the classroom teacher's problems in communication and motivation. There will be no easy solutions to these problems, but one, that of a viable model, has proven valuable in working with youth from other non-White cultures and may be as valuable with these newcomers.

Dr. Marcus Foster illustrated that a viable model or leadership figure is vitally important in helping youth succeed. Usually the most important and most dominant is a family figure—father, mother, sister, brother, or a more distant relative. This model is often so close that it unconsciously plays an important role in helping one to develop attitudes conducive to success in lower economic groups.

During adolescence, youth are likely to seek models outside the family arena. Models are identified as heroes. These heroes must be successful in the eyes of the youth and must be ones with whom youth can identify. They must have a certain "sparkle," or daringness that excites.

Unfortunately, the successful charismatic hero type likely to come from the ghetto may be operating outside the law. An exception is the athlete. The predominance of Blacks in baseball, basketball, and football must surely be traced to such personalities as Jackie Robinson, the Harlem Globetrotters, and those Black football players beginning with Paul Robeson and others of the late 1930s and the early 1940s whose exploits excited the imagination of youth. Jesse Owens in track and Joe Louis in boxing in-

spired a generation of youth in track and boxing, a great number of whom were from the Black community. These heroes served as models for youth of many different ethnic backgrounds, but particularly for the Black youth because they saw someone like themselves who had become successful. The pioneering Black athlete provided a symbol of success developed by an individual based on physical power. This development of self-power ranged from boxing to football, basketball, tennis, and golf and was the result of tremendous self-discipline and training that served as a model for others desiring to follow their example.

In the Black community, the illiterate as well as the intellectual followed the feats of athletes as they represented a breakthrough of barriers hitherto unbroken. During the decade of the thirties they hailed the success of Joe Louis and winced at his verbal expressions. The world followed the records broken by Owens and sympathized with him when he was snubbed by Hitler. These athletes set the stage for Branch Rickey, manager of the Brooklyn Dodgers, to bring Jackie Robinson into professional baseball over the objections of many players and managers. Robinson's phenomenal feats opened the door for a host of other athletes. Football was one of the few sports that accepted minority athletes in the early years. Fritz Pollard and Paul Robeson, Blacks, and Jim Thorpe, an Indian, were among those who made history. Basketball, like baseball, saw little integration until after World War II. The Harlem Globetrotters, active before World War II, were as much artists as athletes in their ball handling and thrilled crowds across the country and later the world. The more elite sports of tennis and golf have only recently opened their doors to the minority athlete. Althea Gibson and Arthur Ashe in tennis and Lee Trevino and Lee Elder in golf are among the best athletes in these sports.

The point is that in areas were one sees success by someone who comes from a similar background, there is more likelihood to try and to be willing to explore that field. Athletics offer an exotic example of this kind of success. Baseball, football, and basketball, in particular, have a larger percentage of players who come from minority backgrounds than most other fields of endeavor. Success is tied, to some degree, with one's willingness to make an attempt in a particular area or media, and to the degree that one is familiar with a particular subject or technique. Nicolaides recognized this when he pointed out that one could usually draw best what was well known, whether an artist or not; a golfer would draw a golf club and a sailor a sail because these were things with which they had real experience, that they had touched and used.[2]

Opportunities to explore and experience a variety of materials often depend upon one's economic background. There is a general assumption that youth from more affluent backgrounds have greater opportunities to travel and see more things than those from poor economic backgrounds, whereas those from the lower economic brackets are permitted to roam without parental guidance and to play in the mud, touching and feeling materials that the more protected children are prevented from experiencing. These assumptions have usually been based on studies concerned with the average child. Art teachers cannot rely on averages, since they must deal with specific children, and averages do not hold for each child. Values of families contain taboos, which permit or prevent exploration in some materials, that override general assumptions. Parents sometimes forbid their children the experience with materials because they will get dirty. These parents may be encouraged to relax such restrictions when shown successful artists as models, who work in materials that parents forbid their children to use, and with whom the parent can relate.

Artists from different ethnic backgrounds can serve as potent models for youth in much the same manner as athletes have. This does not assume that one relates only to models from one's own ethnic background. Indeed, it would be dangerous and would defeat the ultimate aim of education, if this were the case. Certainly this is not the case with athletes, as the box offices indicate. Many more Whites than Blacks follow the exploits of Hank Aaron, Muhammed Ali, or the Black football and basketball players and more Whites than Mexican-Americans are thrilled with the golf of Lee Trevino.

Figure 4.7   John Wilson. *Mother and Child.* Reproduced by the courtesy of John Wilson and from the collection of the Museum of the National Center of Afro-American Artists.

2.   Kimon Nicolaides, *The Natural Way to Draw* (Boston: Houghton Mifflin Company, 1941) p. 6.

The problems posed by the Supreme Court's decision of 1954 and the subsequent integration of races in the schools made the job of the art teacher, seeking models with whom all students could relate, more difficult. The increased influx of greater numbers of immigrants from the "Third world" added to this difficulty. Recent wars, where American military were stationed in countries barely known or unheard of by many United States citizens, has generated interest in people of these countries and influenced them to migrate to the United States. Scientific discoveries, moon shots, and television programs showing the way of life in the United States have added to this desire to migrate to the United States. Although the majority of immigrants still come from Europe and are of the majority, it is interesting to note the following breakdown of the minority population.

The 1970 census gives the total national population as 203,235,298 and within this were 22,580,289 Blacks. Some militant groups believe the actual population to be at least 30 million. The native American Indian population numbered 791,839 up from the 1890 figure of 248,253. The Japanese numbered at 591,290;the Chinese at 435,062, and the Filipino at 343,060. The Jewish population is estimated as 6,060,000, and the Spanish, reported under "origin of population by age and sex," includes all Spanish-speaking people from Mexico, Puerto Rico, Spain, Cuba, and other Latin American countries. This population, classified as "White," numbered at 9,178,000 or 4.5% of the total population.

Ethnic Differences

It cannot be too strongly emphasized that neither the White, Black, Brown, Red, nor Yellow populations are monolithic units that respond in like manner to similar stimuli. A good example is the makeup of the Spanish population, which is really a collection of a variety of cultures and classified under one language. The European "Spanish" is quite different from the Mexican "Spanish" where the mixture of Indian and European sprinkled with African created the Mestizo. The strong Indian influence is seen in the features of modern Mexicans and cultural influences are quite evident. The Cuban culture is again

quite different, although the language is similar, and the African mixture is even greater. Puerto Rican culture is again different from that of Mexico or Spain and the same can be said of the Spanish-speaking countries of South America. Each of these countries have a language relationship but vary in cultural origins.

The Black population originally came from equally, if not more drastically different, cultural backgrounds, but they are more difficult to determine or detect in the present-day population. Originally there were great religious differences among Africans brought to America: Moslem, Christian, and Animist. Slaves were forced to reject previous religious practices and to take that of the master, usually a form of Christianity. Other cultural practices, many requiring use of artifacts, were suppressed and, in the course of time, forgotten. Because of similar conditions, they were forced to relate to and support one another in the face of the "enemy" or "oppressor." They banded together for survival in spite of cultural and language differences. Yet, there remains a residue of differences within the Black community that might be traced to early tribal and cultural differences. One cannot assume that just because a person is Black, that the thoughts and actions of Black people will be the same. Michael Leris emphasizes this in discussing the differences between arts of Black African peoples.

It is equally interesting to note the breakdown of the "White" population, which is even more fragmented and possesses strong ethnic, cultural, and geographic differences. By far, the largest of this group are from English, Scottish, or Welsh origin and make up 14.4% of the total population with a total of 29.5 million. They are followed by Germans with 25.5 million or 12.5%, and the Irish with 16.4 million or 8.0%. The Spanish followed with 9.1 million or 4.5%. The largest category, 85.1 million or 41.6% was under the heading "other." Besides these were Italian, 4.3%, French, 2.6%, Polish, 2.5%, and Russian, 1.1%. Of the 205 million United States citizens 102 million listed their origin in these eight categories. The non-White population—Blacks, American Indian, Japanese, Chinese, and Filipino accounts for 23.9 million of the 85 million listed under the category "other," whereas 17.5 million were not reported under any heading.

The breakdown of age and economic status should

Figure 4.8 Charles Alston. *Black Man, Black Woman, USA.* Reproduced by the courtesy of Charles Alston.

be of interest to teachers. Older persons with fewer children are not as likely to have as many school age children as younger, more prolific ones. Economics tends to determine where and how people live as much as or more than ethnic background.

Persons of English, Scottish or Welsh origin were reported as somewhat older than the national average, with a median age of 33.1 years compared to a national average of 28 years.

They were more likely to have smaller families than the national average but were more likely to be earning more, with a median family income for the family head of $11,350. The national average is $10,359.

The survey indicated there were more immigrants into the United States from Germany—6.8 million—than from any other country between 1820 and 1965.

Persons of German origin had a median income of about $11,000 and a median age of 28.9 years.

Among the Irish in the survey there were considerably more women than men, with 90 men

of Irish origin for every 100 women. The median age was 30.9 years.

Persons of Spanish origin had the lowest median age of any group at 20.1 years and families were larger than the national average, with 57 percent containing four or more persons. The median income, $7,600, was lowest of any of the eight groups.

Persons of Italian origin were among those with the highest median income at $11,646.

Persons of Russian origin had the highest median age, 39.7 years and also the highest family income at $13,929.[3]

Analysis of these figures seems to indicate that: (1) one might be more likely to encounter youth of English, Scottish, or Welsh origin in the classroom because they comprise the largest percentage of the population; (2) youth of the Spanish group are also likely to be encountered as families are larger but they are more likely to be found in the lower economic areas because the median income was the lowest of the eight groups reported; (3) because more immigrants had come from Germany than any other country between 1820 and 1965, there is likelihood of encountering youth from this background; and (4) Russians and Italians, having the highest family income are not as likely to be found in the inner-city or poor neighborhoods as are the Spanish who have the lowest family income of the eight groups.

This survey did not identify non-Whites. The combined non-White population, listed above as 23.9 million, includes 22.6 million Blacks, making them by far the largest of the non-White population, and as an ethnic group, larger than most. If the figures are correct, then as a group, Blacks follow the German figure of 25.5 million. If indeed, the figure of 30 million advanced by the militants is valid, the Black population exceeds all ethnic groups. At any rate, the generally accepted 11% of population figure should be sufficient to support the need for understanding of their cultural heritage. Although they originally came from a variety of cultures, the American experience has forced and welded the Afro-American into one culture, more than any group of immigrants.

3. "Origins of Americans Surveyed," *Arizona Republic,* 13 May 1973.

5 Ethnics and Art Heritage

The term ethnic has been used in a variety of ways to indicate certain people, but has not been pinned down by definition. It is now time to define the term.

Webster's New World Dictionary defines *ethnic* as follows: "1. of nations or groups neither Christian nor Jewish; heathen. 2. designating or of any of the basic groups or divisions of mankind, . . . as distinguished by customs, characteristics, language, . . . etc."[1] *The Reader's Digest Great Encyclopedic Dictionary* gives similar definitions but reverses the order: "1. of belonging to, or distinctive of a particular racial, cultural or language division of mankind; also of or belonging to a population subdivision marked by common features of language, customs, etc. Of or belonging to a people neither Jewish or Christian; heathen; pagan."[2]

The Webster definition is found in the volume copyrighted in 1974 and the *Reader's Digest Great Encyclopedic Dictionary* bears a 1968 copyright. The different positions suggest a change in emphasis on the concept from being "neither Christian nor Jewish" but "heathen" to that of belonging to a distinct or particular racial, cultural, or language division of mankind. The former emphasis concentrated mainly on religion of the "ethnic" being neither Christian nor Jewish, whereas the second couches religion within culture as religion, not mentioned per se, as an important facet of culture.

Ethnic Migrations

What affect does ethnic heritage have upon one's aesthetic expression? More specifically, can the effect of heritage be noted in the work of twentieth-century artists of the United States? Does the aesthetic production of one person, when filtered through the ethnic experience, vary from one of another ethnic background in terms of style and content? Do sociological, economic, and political pressures effect the art produced by people on different sides of the power lines of societal control? If there is indeed an effect caused by ethnic heritage, how deep and how long lasting is such an affect? Can it be probed or measured? Is there a relationship between observable ethnic content in one's work and the time one has been away from the original culture, ancestors, or from the country of origin? Is there a relationship between ethnicity and the ghetto? Is there a lessening of ethnic influence the longer one is from the country of origin? Is there a lessening of ethnicity the longer one is separated from the ethnic ghetto? Have barriers—covert or overt, imagined or real, economic, social, or physical, racial or not— existed preventing some people from crossing such barriers while providing avenues of escape for others? Does an aesthetic mainstream exist in the United States in the twentieth century?

1. From *Webster's New World Dictionary of the American Language,* 2d ed., p. 481. Copyright 1974 by William Collins & World Publishing Company, Inc., Cleveland, Ohio. Reprinted by permission of the publisher.

2. *The Reader's Digest Great Encyclopedic Dictionary,* 3rd ed. (1968), p. 455. Reprinted by permission of the publisher from the *Reader's Digest Great Encyclopedic Dictionary,* © 1966, 1968, 1971 The Reader's Digest Association, Inc.

Figure 5.1 Jacob Lawrence. *Northbound.* 1962. Tempera, 24 x 30 inches. Reproduced by the courtesy of Jacob Lawrence.

In the search of answers to these questions, a number of avenues might be taken, but there is no certainty that any one avenue or combination of avenues will give definite or complete answers. I have chosen to pursue the avenue of history concerning the origins of population and settlement. This avenue explores migrations of populations from different parts of the world into the United States and explains some of the attitudes that might conceivably affect aesthetic products.

The central part of North America, the United States, is generally considered to have been unknown prior to its "discovery" by Christopher Columbus

in 1492. There is some dispute, claiming that Leif Ericson preceded Columbus by over 500 years. Others claim that the Mali king, Abubakari II (brother of Mansa Musa), led a fleet of 2,000 ships that sailed from the west coast of Africa headed for the Americas in the fourteenth century. The meaning of "unknown" obviously means unknown to Europeans. If Ericson did precede Columbus, there is little evidence that he remained to colonize the land nor did he later send his countrymen to do so. That is, unless some of the people Columbus encountered were Norwegians. This is highly unlikely since the history of most of the people found in the

country has been traced hundreds of years prior to either Columbus or Ericson. The fate of the fleet from Mali is unknown, but some scholars, such as Floyd Hayes, have recently attempted to compare certain physical forms and cultural practices found in America with those of peoples of the west coast of Africa. Hayes cites that theories regarding the presence of Africans in pre-Columbian America are not new and supports his statement with references from De Roo in 1900, Wiener in 1920, Von Hagen in 1957, Lawrence in 1962, Reinert in 1967, and Davis in 1970.[3]

There is one dubious contribution made by Columbus that will perhaps always remain, for better or worse. Columbus thought he had reached India, land of the spices for which he was searching, and called the people he saw "Indians," a term that remains in common usage to identify these native Americans, who have since been known as Indians. A few, such as the Eskimo, may not be officially classified as Indian. With the statehood of Alaska, as with Hawaii, the inhabitants of these territories became citizens of the United States and numbered among those whose heritage did not stem from Europe.

There is no argument that the area now known as the United States was populated by the people called Indians. If there were any others, they were either not in significant numbers or they left no trace of their existence. Columbus had no way of knowing about the vast differences of language and cultural patterns between those he found living in America. Subsequent populations of this vast area of naturally beautiful territory came in waves, mainly from Europe and Africa. A few came from the Far East, Japan, and China, and fewer still from the Near East, South Seas, and India. In the early years surprisingly few seemed to come from south of the Mexican border. The original inhabitants of Central and South America, as well as the coastal islands, were also classified as Indians. An assault, similar to that of the Northern Hemisphere, was being made on these countries. Added to this was the introduction of the slave trade, where human beings in chains were forcibly removed from Africa and brought to all parts of the Americas, from Canada to Argentina,

Figure 5.2 Unknown artist. Head of a cane. Wood, from Senufo. Reproduced by the courtesy of the author.

44

3. Floyd Hayes, "The African Presence in America Before Columbus," *Black World* 22, no. 9 (Chicago: Johnson Publishing Company, 1973):4-11.

Figure 5.3 Unknown artist. Mask. Brass, from the Bamun people, Cameroon, West Africa. Reproduced by courtesy of the author.

with the largest number being concentrated in the Caribbean, the United States, and Brazil. The Caribbean Islands overflowed with slaves, as this was the holding area before they were sent to other countries, and subsequently those of African heritage became the majority population of many of these islands.

The Spanish, among the earliest settlers, came in small numbers in the early sixteenth century. The English followed in larger numbers in the next century. After the Europeans, Africans provided the second largest migration. The first recorded ones came with Columbus in 1492. One, Pedro Niño, has been identified as a member of his crew. The Spanish brought slaves to their first settlements as early as 1526. In 1538, Estivanico, a Black from Spain, who was possibly a slave, led an expedition from Mexico into the north that discovered Arizona and New Mexico. In 1619, the first slaves landed in Jamestown, Virginia.

Although a majority of slaves came from the west coast of Africa, there was a significant number of slaves, who came from the interior of the continent and from the east coast. Most of these were Black people who lived south of the Sahara Desert. Nobody knows exactly how many of these Blacks were forcibly brought from Africa to the Americas, although several estimates have been made from the data available. Basil Davidson has estimated that the Portugese carried no fewer than a million slaves to Brazil between 1580 and 1680 and that the British colonies in North America and the Caribbean received more than two million in the following hundred years. For the grand total of slaves landed alive in the lands across the Atlantic, an eminent student of population statistics, Kuczynski, came to the conclusion that fifteen million might be a conservative figure. Other writers have accepted this as a minimal figure; some have thought that the probable total was about fifty million, and still others believe it was much higher than this.[4] The magnitude of the African influx can be understood when compared with the total 1870 population of the United States of 38.5 million. Davidson grimly reminds us that

. . . the sum of all the slaves landed alive was not, of course, the total of those embarked. Many died in the dreaded Middle passage . . . Out of

146,799 captives that were bought in Africa on 541 slaving voyages from the Port of Nantes in the years 1748-1782, only 127,133 were actually sold. The difference is 13 per cent, and most of this difference must have been caused by death during the ocean crossing."[5]

Origins of slaves brought to America were listed by tribal names as countries did not then exist. They came from a number of kingdoms and city-states headed by powerful chieftans. In discussing those who were brought, Davidson claims that barely a single tribal name was missing from the records. He also tells us that there were said to be as many as twenty thousand slaves in Mexico as early as 1570.[6]

Most of the Africans who came to Mexico in those early days were probably of the Mande group of people who lived then, as they still do, in the lands behind the far west bulge of the Guinea Coast. These captives were generally known as Mandingos, and the word "Mandingo" has survived in Mexico as the popular name for devil. But the careful records of the Inquisition in Mexico, which were kept as part of the process of "safeguarding Christianity" by ensuring baptism, show that the land was fertilized by many African peoples.

Some of these were brought into the country not under their own names but under those their captors knew them by. Thus Nupe captives who were taken and traded by the Yoruba people of western Nigeria were generally called Tapas, and as such they were delivered by the traders to the markets of the New World. In their turn the Yoruba, enslaved by the Fon people of Dahomey to the west of them, were known as Nagos, and entered America under that name. The Susu people from the coast of the modern Republic of Guinea do not appear in the Mexican records; instead they were registered under Xoxo. Bambara captives from the Middle Niger were known to the Inquisition as Bumbura; the Tuculor of Senegal

4. Basil Davidson, *The African Slave Trade* (Boston: Little, Brown and Company, 1961), p. 79. By permission of Little, Brown and Company, in association with the Atlantic Monthly Press.

5. Ibid.

6. Ibid., p. 103.

as Tucuxui; the numerous Foulah or Fulani, under various labels, and derivations. Among tribal names that suffered no distortion one may note the Kissi and Senufu, who came from the lands of the forest belt behind the coast of present-day Liberia and the Republic of Guinea.[7]

Although a majority of slaves came from the west coast of Africa, along a 3,000 mile coastline that stretched between Senegal in the north and Angola in the south, a few came from east Africa as early as the sixteenth century.

Those carried from the Mozambique Coast were called Kaffarians, after the Arabic word *Kafir*, meaning pagan . . . "Zoza" slaves in Mexico were probably Xosa from the far southeastern part of south Africa. . . . other victims came from places still farther afield; the Mexican records tell of slaves from Burma, Malaya, Java and even China.[8]

Davidson touches briefly on the survival of indigenous cultural patterns brought by slaves to the New World and he states that they

. . . were often strong and numerous enough to revive and recreate the customs and beliefs of their homelands. Some of the West Indian islands and Brazil show this very clearly; nearly all the slave populated lands of the Americas show it to some extent. Transported to Brazil in large numbers, Yoruba captives evolved a compound of their own beliefs and Christianity. . . . They printed a deep African accent on the everyday culture of the cities of the coast. Thus the *orishas* of the Yoruba—the national gods—have been reborn in Brazilian Bahia as Christian saints. At Rio de Janeiro—the god of war, Ogun, has become St. George, the sainted Knight of the Catholics . . . Yemanja and Oshun, goddesses of the Yoruba, have in their turn become fused with Our Lady of the Conception. . . . Even African languages have survived in some truncated form.[9]

Davidson has given but a glimpse of some remnants of African culture in the New World. Janheinz Jahn digs deeply and comes up with examples of new

forms based on African origins. They are expressed within the context of the part of the New World in which they are found.[10]

Africans brought to the New World vestiges of culture of the various societies from which they came. In some places this package of culture was virtually intact, and when opened, continued much the same as they had known it in the Old World. In other instances, parts of the package of culture were lost or damaged and strains of the old culture were difficult to transplant, especially those parts that had to be carried externally. In those instances where language groups and families remained together, as in Brazil and Surinam, strong traditions of society and art continue. In Surinam, people called Djuka still exist and live much as they did in their native Africa.

Ethnic Components

All people stem from an original heritage. All people are ethnic. As used in general conversation, the impression is often gained that "ethnic" is only a means of identifying members of the minority United States population, such as Indians, Afro-Americans, Mexican-Americans, Oriental-Americans, and Jewish people, and that it refers to first- or second-generation Europeans who are "hyphenated-Americans." Commonly used in certain parts of the United States, the terms Afro-American, Spanish-American, German-American serve to identify the origin of a segment of the population. Such terms begin to lose rational meaning when they are applied to persons originally from the American continent, such as Canadian-American or Mexican-American. The term Canadian-American is seldomly used, but Mexican-American is common and refers to a United States citizen, who is either naturalized or has ancestors that came from Mexico. Since Mexico is a sovereign country of North America, is not the citizen of Mexico also a

7. Ibid.
8. Ibid.
9. Ibid.
10. Janheinz Jahn, *Muntu* (New York: Grove Press, Inc., 1961).

Figure 5.4 Jacob Lawrence. *Piano Lesson*. Gouache. Reproduced by courtesy of Jacob Lawrence and from the collection of the New Jersey State Museum.

Mexican-American? Since Canada is a soverign country of North America, could the Canadian whose ancestors migrated from Italy also be an Italian-American? Would the Mexican, whose ancestors came from Poland, be a Polish-American or must he be a Polish-Mexican-American? Could it be due to difficulties of pronouncing the name of the country, the United States, as it might be coupled with a country of origin? It would be awkward to say "Afro-United States," or "Afro-Statesan." Through the use of such terms we have unconsciously "colonized" other countries to the degree that citizens of the United States have usurped the use of the word "America" for themselves and thereby denied the "American-ness" of other countries of the American continent. If this is so, could this be a contributing, however subtle, cause of the identity crisis affecting some youth? Could this be a reason, perhaps

unconscious in intent, behind the insistence of militant youth of Mexican heritage to call themselves "Chicano"?

When opened, the ethnic shell reveals an amazing variety of kernels. The native American, a term often applied to that group designated by Columbus as "Indians," is made up of vastly differing cultures. Societies, such as the Seneca, the Kiowa, the Pima, the Kwakiutl, the Hopi, and the Navajo, developed life-styles, governmental values, languages, and arts that differed greatly from one another. There also were many overlapping patterns of culture which they shared over the centuries. Some similarities occurred because they were humans living on the same continent coming into contact and therefore influencing one another. But many acts and expressions appear to be similar only to the uninitiated, the insensitive, and unobserving persons who bring their own preconceived ideas of how a group of people should act or react. Obviously, trade, war, marriage, and the normal contact of people within similar geographic boundaries will tend to create similarities as they have in Europe, Africa, and Asia; but the essence of ethnicity lies in the different cultural groups within the large continents.

There appear to be certain underlying similarities of culture, actions, and art between the Indian peoples of the Americas that set them apart from peoples of other parts of the world. In the same sense, peoples of western Europe are similar to one another in spite of sharp cultural and language differences. The same observation can be made of people living within the continental confines of Africa, Asia, the South Seas, and the Orient. Natural boundaries seem to provide perimeters beyond which the mass of people did not extend to any great degree, and centuries of contact and exchange between peoples of the continent gave rise to some basic concepts that are reflected in a type of life-style, religion, and

aesthetic expression, differing greatly from that developed on other continents. To be sure, vast differences exist between peoples of these continents but they are more similar to one another than they are to those of any other continent. One of the major and more delightful differences is found in the food and methods of preparing different foods.

Culinary Arts   The delightful aromas of food prepared according to ethnic dictates can be experienced throughout the United States. On a warm summer evening, the Manhattan Islander, who rides in a bus with an opened window from Greenwich Village to Harlem, or from the eastside to the westside of the island, will experience many different aromas from kitchens of the neighborhoods. On Manhattan Island, one can find small enclaves of ethnic populations, clinging to a style of living reflecting aspects of life in the Old World. Much pride is taken in one's ethnic background, particularly when it comes to food. Restaurant signs attest to this and indicate that

Figure 5.5   A Chinese restaurant.

Figure 5.6   A Greek restaurant.

Figure 5.7 A Mexican bakery and restaurant.

Chinese, Mexican, French, German, Italian, Spanish (which differs somewhat from Mexican), and "soul" food, a euphemism for Afro-American, is served. Differences for taste in food may also suggest a difference in taste in the arts, such as music, dance, literature, and the visual arts. It would be of significant interest for research studies to examine the relationships that may or may not exist in the choice of food and the manner of its preparation and the handling of space, line, form, hue, value, texture, pattern, rhythm, sounds, and all the elements that make up the arts as influenced by ethnic cultures.

It must not be assumed that folkways and ethnic attitudes remain with individuals after several generations of living in the United States and that in time all ethnic attitudes dissipate or disappear altogether. Some facets of ethnic origin remain longer than one realizes and many are constantly refueled by newly arrived immigrants and by return visits to the motherland. One large area of ethnic tenacity concerns taste, particularly culinary tastes and preferences for a particular manner of food preparation.

Mexican food is a delicacy in the Southwest. Signs advertising German, French, and Italian food give some indication of ethnic culinary preferences of the community. Soul food, comprised of inexpensive ingredients, is likely to be found in Black neighborhoods. The availability of foods in differents parts of the country and kinds of ethnic stress on preparation

may be closely related to the origins of the Americans who live in these communities. It is no surprise that a major menu of the United States includes meat and potatoes, a basic fare of the English, Welsh, Scots, and Germans.

Slaves were given the leavings, or what the masters did not want, on many plantations. They had to make do with this food and, just as today, the economically poor have had to devise ways of making limited food supplies as tasty as possible. Mexican food and soul food are the result of the creativity of each group. Exotic foods are called exotic because they are unfamiliar to the majority of the population, and they can be found in larger cities where immigrants cluster in ghetto neighborhoods.

The general population often delights in sampling foods from various parts of the world either in restaurants or at home. But everyday fare is likely to be based on tastes formed at home. Taste choices range from spicy to bland, and the basis for these choices are formed at an early age. An hypothesis that needs research for substantiation suggests that the hotter the climate, the spicier or hotter the food, and the colder the climate, the less spicy the food. A Mexican meal is usually much too hot for most English people, yet Mexican dishes are quite mild in comparison with those of Nigeria or Indonesia.

This matter of taste may stem from methods of food preservation. Refrigeration is a relatively recent invention and food spoils in hot climates much quicker than in colder climates. Spices, pepper, sugar, and salt act as preservatives and cover up the taste of food that is near or at the point of spoiling. Then too, sugarcane, peppers, and spices are more likely to be found growing in warmer climates, and persons inhabiting these regions have grown accustomed, over the centuries, to generous use of such spices in food preparation. I have found Mexican dishes to be much more spicy than those I had become accustomed to from a childhood in North Carolina, but nevertheless I found them palatable. In a Nigerian village restaurant I found even the mildest food available too hot to swallow without tears and excessive pain. On the other hand, I found most food prepared for British taste, whether in London or Nairobi, to be so bland to my palate that it was practically tasteless. In the matter of taste in food choices as in other tastes, what may be the delight of one person may be repugnant to another.

The manner in which food is prepared differs from one ethnic group to another and is not limited to the spiciness or lack of it. The way it looks and smells, as well as its taste is important. Color, texture, pattern, arrangement, and mixture of ingredients on the dish or dishes is also important. Gumbo, for example, is a mixture of okra, rice, shrimp, fish, or other meat, and a variety of other ingredients, depending on the cook's creativity and what is available. It is a delight to the olfactory and visual senses of those who like gumbo, but repugnant to those unaccustomed to having foods mixed and cooked together.

The manner in which food is served and eaten has ethnic connotations similar to those of preparation. In some cultures the noise made while eating attests to the enjoyment of the food. In others, to make audible noises while eating indicates a lack of good manners. To eat with the fingers is considered barbaric by some, but to others it is the acceptable way of eating. Although humans are physically constructed the same way, the Aesop fable of the fox and the crane, who are built differently, symbolizes dramatically some of the cultural differences between people. For the fox and the crane the choice of vessels in which to serve food was a matter of form and function. The fox could manage food in a plate but not in a vase, and the crane preferred food served in a tall vase where its beak had maximum efficiency.

Within the Ethnic Shell   The different kernels within the ethnic shell are at times harmonious and at other times hostile to one another. Often they are strongly flavored by other forces, such as religion. Christianity and its many forms, Catholic and Protestant; Jewish; Moslem; animist; Buddhist; Hindu; Shinto; and other religious expressions help determine taste preferences and shape cultural expressions. Religion is basic to ethnicity and contributes to either harmony or hostility within the geographic confines of a country. Examples of such hostilities are seen in Ireland between Catholics and Protestants, in Nigeria between Yoruba and Ibo, and in the Middle East between Jews and Arabs. Harmonious examples are less explosive than hostile ones and therefore less obvious. They represent peaceful exchange within the ethnic shell.

Hostilities occur between peoples of the same geographic area for reasons other than religion.

Hostilities may have ethnic roots, such as between the Walloons and Flemish in Belgium who speak different languages and may have political reasons, such as in North and South Vietnam, North and South Korea and East and West Germany.

Image-makers of the media, novelists, and wishful thinkers have long projected the United States as a melting pot of peoples who shed their strong ethnic backgrounds and become alike in feelings, attitudes, and expressions. The European immigrants came expecting differences of class to melt away, and for some this has happened. Immigrants from the British Isles and western Europe have seemingly melted or have mixed among themselves more than they have mixed with people coming from other continents. There are indications that the Spanish and the French were more prone to mix with the native Americans and Africans than were the English. This social structure, with its taboos, has provided a major barrier to intermixing of ethnic groups. Upward economic mobility has often opened the door to social mobility. This mobility has been more readily available to those of European background than to others.[11]

Language   The broader definition relating to race, culture, and language seem more appropriate for the discussion of definition of ethnics. Many cultural anthropologists, however, reject "race" as a valid division of mankind as being overly simplistic or impossible to measure with any degree of accuracy. Language and culture remain as important guideposts of ethnic understanding.

The language one speaks is relatively easy to detect, as are variations of the standard usage of that language. On the other hand, a language may be replete with slang or idiomatic expressions that vary from the standard usage and this makes it difficult for people who speak the same language to understand one another. Standard English, as spoken in the United States, is a good example of a language with many variations.

The fact that English is referred to as the "mother tongue" indicates the ethnic heritage of the majority population. The syntax, rhythm, and manner of speaking English in the United States is quite different from the way it is spoken in England. During

11.   Harvey Zorbaugh, *The Gold Coast and the Slum* (Chicago: University of Chicago Press, 1929).

the Brussels World Exposition, I taught art at the Children's Creative Center located in the United States Pavilion. This unique center was sponsored by the Museum of Modern Art under the direction of Victor D'Amico. After several weeks of working with children from many parts of the world we became fairly adept in identifying the country from which the children came and the language they spoke. Clues of their origin were given by mode of dress, body movements, and snatches of conversation. Occasionally we did not hear them talk before they were brought into the painting room, and this made our little guessing game more exciting, as many children were shy and would not speak unless spoken to first. One youth looked and acted as though he might be English or from the United States, so I asked him if he spoke English and he shook his head in the negative and said "No." I asked the same question in French, German, and Flemish, and each time received the same answer. Other teachers asked if he spoke Spanish, Italian, Danish, or Swedish, and each time the answer was the same, "No!" In desperation I blurted out, "What language do you speak?" And he answered, "I speak American." He taught me an important lesson—there is a great difference between the "English" spoken in England and that spoken in the United States. This difference becomes clearer as one listens to the speech of people in London streets or pubs, and one realizes how mixed or "American" our speech has become.

The first settlers who came from England no doubt spoke the "standard English" of their day and lo-cale, but soon they set foot on new land and began to exchange words and ideas with the Indians and later with settlers from France, Holland, and Ger-many. The nature of spoken English in North America began to change. The musical speech patterns of African slaves modulated the cadence of English spoken in southern states. Words, phrases, patterns, rhythms, intonations, and syntax of spoken English varied according to the influences of other languages. French was the official language in Louisiana until its purchase in 1803, after which time it became the *unofficial* language. Even today French, or a patois of French and English, is still spoken by many.

Examples of unique variations or accents of spoken English are to be found across the United States, and some provincial speech is difficult for outsiders

Figure 5.8 Samella Lewis. *Boy with Flute*. 1968. Oil, 30 x 15 inches. Reproduced by courtesy of Samella Lewis.

to understand. The "broad A" of Bostonians, the western drawl, "Brooklynese" as spoken in Brooklyn, and the southern drawl with its many different patterns from Virginia to Texas are but a few. The speech patterns of the people of Sea Islands, located off the coast of South Carolina and Georgia and largely inhabited by slave descendants, are said to resemble sixteenth century or Elizabethan English.

Although language might be considered a major factor of ethnic identification, the purity of the language varies and tends to blend with other languages and speech patterns more in urban than in rural or isolated mountainous or desert areas. Formal language education, radio, and television tend to accelerate the blending of speech patterns into a homogenous expression and reduces the unique variations.

Resistance to this homogeneity has grown in recent years. "Black English," a concept unheard of as late as 1960, has gained support in many quarters, particularly among the young and militant. It is now even taught in some schools. The concept has been rejected or strongly resisted mainly by older and more conservative people who see this as a divisive technique to further limit the ability of Black youth to succeed in the mainstream. Chicano youth speak Spanish among themselves at school, even though it is often a punishable offense in many schools. Young militant Indian youth clamor to preserve their native languages and some schools now instruct in the language native to the community during the early grades. This desire for the preservation or the creation of "ethnic" languages is an extension of group identification, and a way to preserve a culture and maintain unique differences but not necessarily to substitute as the major official language. It may well be a means of preserving the ethnic culture.

Race Race has long been thought to be a major identifying factor of the ethnic component. Color of skin, texture and color of hair, color of eyes, and shape of head have been the factors most often used in identifying race. Simplistic definitions, unfortunately, still are adhered to by many people who lump mankind into White, Black, Red, Yellow, and Brown peoples. Definitions of race tend to shift from one publication to another and from one time to another. The second edition of the *Columbia Encyclopedia* stated that the concept of race, based on skin color, hair texture, head shape, and other conspicuous physical features as a division of humanity was obsolete, but the third edition carries no mention of this division being obsolete.

Although a large body of literature on racial origins exists, many ideas have become generally accepted regardless of the fact that there is very little direct evidence on which to base conclusions. This point is supported by Ralph Linton in *The Tree of Culture,* in which he traces theories of the development of man and conclusions reached by physical and cultural anthropologists. Linton concludes that

> racial differences seem to have had little or no effect on human history. Their present significance is almost entirely social; i.e., the individual's physical characteristics are significant only so far as they mark him as a member of a particular social group. . . . Apparently, the members of any racial group can assume any culture in which they are reared . . . and we know that members of all the great racial stocks have made important additions to culture.[12]

Classification by race continues to be made in census reports, school records, legal documents and certificates, and in dictionaries and encyclopedias. *Webster's New World Dictionary* defines race:

> 1. any of the different varieties of mankind, distinguished by form of hair, color of skin and eyes, stature, bodily proportions, etc.: many anthropologists now consider that there are only three primary major groups, the Caucasoid, Negroid, and Mongoloid, each with various subdivisions (sometimes also called *races*): the term has acquired so many unscientific connotations that in this sense it is often replaced in scientific usage by *ethnic stock or group* 2. a population that differs from others in the relative frequency of some gene or genes: a modern scientific use 3. any geographical, national, or tribal ethnic grouping 4. a) the state of belonging to a certain ethnic stock, group, etc. b) the qualities, traits, etc. belonging, or supposedly belonging, to such a category 5. any group of people having the same ancestry; family; clan; lineage 6. any group of people having the same activities, habits, ideas, etc. . . .[13]

12. Ralph Linton, *The Tree of Culture* (New York: Alfred Knopf, 1955), p. 28.
13. From *Webster's New World Dictionary of the American Language,* 2d ed., p. 1169. Copyright 1974 by William Collins + World Publishing Company, Inc., Cleveland, Ohio. Reprinted by permission of the publisher.

Figure 5.9   Hale Woodruff. *The Art of the Negro,* "Native Forms." Mural, panel one. The art of the African manifested itself in a diversity of forms, styles, and materials. Here are hunters disguised as birds and animals; mask forms, sculptors at work; stone carving; cave painting. Reproduced by courtesy of Hale Woodruff and the Atlanta University and from the collection of the Atlanta University.

Figure 5.10   Hale Woodruff. *The Art of the Negro,* "Interchange." Mural, panel two. The artists of Africa were long in contact with the Greeks, Romans, and Egyptians of antiquity. Here are symbolic columns—Greek, Egyptian, African, and Roman; and sculptural forms. Reproduced by courtesy of Hale Woodruff and the Atlanta University and from the collection of the Atlanta University.

Figure 5.11   Hale Woodruff. *The Art of the Negro,* "Dissipation." Mural, panel three. With the coming of the Europeans to Africa, much of the native culture and art was destroyed. Here is pictured the burning of the great capital of Benin as well as general symbolizing of the looting and plundering. Reproduced by courtesy of Hale Woodruff and the Atlanta University and from the collection of the Atlanta University.

Figure 5.12 Hale Woodruff. *The Art of the Negro,* "Parallels." Mural, panel four. Different groups of people with similar cultural motivation have developed art forms. Here are totemic forms of the North, West, and American Indian. Reproduced by courtesy of Hale Woodruff and the Atlanta University and from the collection of the Atlanta University.

According to the first definition and to the U.S. Census Bureau, the major racial identifications of the United States are between "Caucasian" and "Negro," or Black and White. The census identification by race also includes Indian, Japanese, Chinese, and Filipino. A separate category for the Jewish population is given by cities whereas the other populations are listed by states and cities. The Spanish-speaking population which includes the Americans of Mexican, Cuban, and Puerto Rican descent is listed under "white."[14]

The largest minority ethnic population of the United States is Negro or Black. Their physical features include a wide range of hair textures, eye colors, and head shapes. These vary from skin colors of black to white, hair from kinky to straight, every eye color imaginable and sometimes a different color for each eye, a variety of head shapes, and statures from short to very tall. The net result is that it is impossible to identify all Negroes or Black people by physical characteristics alone. In fact, there are many Black people who are whiter than many Whites, whose hair texture is straighter, and whose eyes are bluer.

The Negro of the United States has been defined as any person with a drop of African or Negro blood. This definition is obviously an outgrowth of the slave trade. It served to identify slaves and any offspring of slaves and Whites. After slavery and during the Reconstruction period it was enforced as an effort to keep former slaves in economic servitude and to disenfranchise them. The results have

14. *The World Almanac and Book of Facts,* George E. Delury, ed. (New York: Newspaper Enterprises Association, 1974).

Figure 5.13 Hale Woodruff. *The Art of the Negro,* "In-fluences." Mural, panel five. The impact of African art on the works of modern artists. Reproduced by courtesy of Hale Woodruff and the Atlanta University and from the collection of the Atlanta University.

been that there are many White-looking Black people, who have been raised in the Black community and are ethnically Black.

One of the most striking examples of such a person was Walter White, formerly executive secretary of the National Association of Colored People (NAACP), who helped to mold this organization into a powerful political force. He was a man of fair skin, wavy hair, and blue eyes. In his autobiography, *A Man Called White,* he writes that he took the job with the NAACP after the death of his father, who was also of fair complexion. White's father had been injured in an automobile accident in Atlanta, Georgia, where the family lived. The father was taken to the emergency room of the "White" hospital and the family was alerted. Some members of the family, who rushed to the scene, were not so "White" and upon seeing that Mr. White was actually Black, he was denied entrance to the

"White" hospital and ordered transferred to the "Black" one. The time that elapsed during the transfer from one hospital to another and the lack of attendance caused the death of the father and left the son embittered.

I have personal recollections of Walter White telling of the incident. He was my mother's college classmate and had been invited to speak at the high school where my father was principal and was our houseguest, because at that time few hotels in the South permitted Black people to spend the night and none of these could be considered first, or even second class. I listened, spellbound, to his adventures as he recounted stories about lynching that he heard from the enemy who thought he was White. Some of his adventures would pale the exploits of the most daring television or movie detective.

The absurdity of racial classification in the United States would be amusing if it were not so tragic.

Many Black people, who look White, have "passed" over into the White community. Some have become quite prominent and are known, but not officially recognized, by their Black relatives whom they periodically visit for a bit of soul food or other cultural trappings. There are others, however, who are so afraid of discovery and loss of position that they become more racist than the worst White bigot. George S. Schuyler has written an amusing and biting novel, *Black No More,* which is a parody on the situation.

Personally, I am unaware of any racial situation that is comparable to that of the United States as it relates to the color line. This is not to say that problems of people of African heritage are not as great or even greater in other countries, even in some countries on the African continent, it is the attitude and the effect of racial attitudes on the non-White as well as on the White population that is degrading and demeaning to all. This attitude and the resulting separation and degradation is not limited to Black people but extends to all minorities, Indians, Mexican-Americans, Puerto Ricans, and Cubans. The worst effect is that it robs one of self-esteem and feelings of self-worth.

In Brazil I was told that I would be considered White but in the United States would never be so mistaken, even if it was desired. The composer, William A. Dawson, told an amusing story of an experience he had some years ago in Spain. Dawson, a Black, was the guest at a dinner party, and the host asked him about the Negroes in the United States. The composer explained that one drop of Negro blood would make you a Negro in the United States. The host, after thoughtful silence, broke out in uncontrollable laughter and when asked the reason for his mirth, he exclaimed with a sweep of his hand that included all at the table, "under that definition, we are all Negroes!"

One evening in Brussels my wife and I were the dinner guests of an engineer whose daughter-in-law worked with us at the Children's Creative Center. After dinner, when social barriers had been relaxed, the host turned to us and asked, "Who are these Negroes we hear so much about?" and we replied, "We are the Negroes." They found this difficult to believe. Another incident, this time at home, reveals the complexity of the problem. My wife, a biology teacher in an inner-city school, made up mostly of Black and Chicano students and where racial troubles had flared, told her class in passing conversation that she had been Black for all the fifty years of her life. Even some of the Black students were surprised as she is one of those fair-complexioned Black people.

The slogan, "Black is beautiful" followed closely the cry "Black power" during the early 1960s. I used the slogan as a departure for a discussion of design and to bolster self-image in a lecture given to students and faculty at Ahmadu Bello University in Zaria, Nigeria. In a light and jocular vein I explained, in terms of design, why "Black is beautiful." The condition of beauty, I explained, requires variety or variation upon a theme. When one observes Black people of the United States, one sees a play upon the human form; there is unity in that form but there is variety of skin complexion from deepest black to whitest white; from hair that is rough and woolly to hair that is straight and smooth, eyes of every color; there is truly a great variety of colors and textures to be found among the American Black population and this makes them beautiful. On the other hand, I jested that in order to be White the variation of skin color and hair texture must be quite limited, and if beauty is based in a complexity of variations, then the American Black is truly beautiful.

It was interesting to note that among Africans the distinctions between European and African seemed to be more important than between Black and White. The importance of skin color, hair texture, eye color, and other physical attributes seems to vary from one African country to another.

Culture Culture, the third and most complex ethnic factor, is defined here as the way of life chosen by a society of people. The *Columbia Encyclopedia* defines culture as:

The customs, ideas, and attitudes shared by a group, which make up its culture, are transmitted from generation to generation by learning processes rather than biological inheritance. . . . Language and other symbolic media are the chief agents of cultural transmission, but many behavior patterns are acquired through experience alone. A pattern of "cultural universals" is found in all societies. It includes such inevitable human institutions as social organization, religion, political structure, economic organization, and material culture (tools, weapons, clothing).[15]

Ralph Linton defines culture as "the mass of behavior that human beings in any society learn from their elders and pass on to the younger generation."[16]

Culture is the pivotal component of ethnicity around which other components may rotate. Culture encompasses language and supercedes race since a number of racial characteristics may be found under the same cultural umbrella. Within the components of culture, two of the most dynamic factors are religion and the arts: visual, auditory, verbal, kinetic, and culinary. Religion and art in most cultures are mutually supportive; the religious message depends upon oratory, music, painting, sculpture, dance, costume, and so forth. Deeds of the holy people are depicted in paintings, sculptures, dances, and costumes. Songs intone the greatness of their deeds and instrumental music creates moods. Dances involve movement of the body and give rhythmic communication with the deities. Costumes, masks, and other paraphernalia accent the scene, and oratory verbalizes deeds and importance of occasions. Religious cosmogony describes the origins of society and establishes cannons of conduct, mores, taboos, and limits of activity touching every phase of everyone's life within the society to shape patterns of culture.

Art and religion are complex components of culture that determine the ethnic form and that need closer examination.

15. From *The Columbia Encyclopedia* (Columbia University Press), p. 490.
16. Linton, *The Tree of Culture*, p. 3.

6 Religion: A Component of Ethnic Art

Religion is a powerful factor in shaping the ethnic component and is responsible for the production of more works of art than either nationality or race, or than intercontinental expressions, if either of these demand the creation of a work of art. Natural forces, such as geographic location, climate, terrain, vegetable and animal life, influence the artist and the art product. Concepts of self, family, clan, tribe, and race play an important part in the final form. But religion, a phenomenon that seems to be basic to all human society, has demanded homage from all the arts; the spoken and written words, visual expressions, vocal and instrumental music, and dance in all its many forms. A great deal of art production has been to promote religion.

Although the first explorers of the New World came for economic reasons, representatives of the church came along with them, and the first settlers came for both economic and religious reasons. Cortez brought Catholicism into the southern part of the continent and the English settlers brought Protestantism into the northern part. Africans brought religious beliefs that were neither Catholic nor Protestant but were equally as strong as either one, and the beliefs they brought were blended with both. The native American Indians had their own strong religious beliefs that differed from any of those of the newcomers. All of these religions had a basic belief in a Supreme Being, but expressions of their beliefs took different forms and some were in opposition to one another. The ethnic nature of each strongly shaped attitudes and influenced the forms that shaped the various arts whether they were religious or secular

in purpose. The northern Europeans, led by the English settlers, came seeking religious freedom. These included people from France, Germany, Moravia, and from eastern European countries as well. Each held strong, if not rigid, ideas about God and worship, and each had some disagreement with the ideas of the others. These differences often became the basis of conflict. Conflicting attitudes were also the basis of fomenting attitudes of superiority, of being "God's Chosen People," and those who thought and acted differently were considered "heathen."

This brief excursion into the "thicket" of religious attitudes held by the three different groups of people making up the population of the United States, Indian, European, and African, may serve as background to understand how different religious beliefs shaped the ethnic nature of this population. There is no intent in this excursion to demean or to extoll religious practices or concepts of any one of the groups concerned, but merely to state a point-of-view that mankind in different parts of the world had developed strong attitudes toward the origin of the species in terms of religion and that these attitudes have influenced the art products.

Ancient Religious Roots

Among the many prehistoric structures in Europe, monumental stone structures appear that may have to do with a cult of the dead or worship of the sun. Stonehenge is perhaps the most impressive of this

Figure 6.1 Lois Mailou Jones. *Veve Vodou III.* 1963. Oil and collage, 29¾ x 38½ inches. Reproduced by courtesy of Lois Mailou Jones.

group. Cave paintings from Altamira, Spain, and Lascaux, France, have left images of animals and men, and researchers have suggested that they were religious in purpose. Similar paintings have been found in the Sahara Desert, in southern Africa, and on the North American continent.

Some of the earliest records of religious worship come from Egypt, where monuments to the various gods have been identified. Sculptures, temples, pyramids, and paintings dedicated to and representative of the various gods still remain giving dramatic evidence of strong religious beliefs, expressed through artistic renderings, in this early civilization.

Some of the earliest forms of writing give information about the life and religion of the Egyptians, and great stress is placed on life after death. A major deity was the sun god Ra, but Osiris ruled life after death. Osiris and Isis had their place in the pantheon of the gods, but Ra the sun god seemed paramount. Diop writes that Ikhnaton, in his attempt to revive the early monotheism that existed in Egypt, possibly influenced Moses by his reform.[1]

1. Cheikh A. Diop, *The African Origins of Civilization: Myth or Reality,* ed. and trans. Mercer Cook (New York: Lawrence Hill and Co., 1974), p. 6.

Herodotus reports that the Greeks were strongly influenced by the Egyptian gods. Greek mythology, with its long list of gods who freely fraternized with humans, has strongly influenced the Western arts, such as drama, literature, sculpture, and painting. The Romans succeeded the Greeks and took over their gods with the addition of some of their own. At the height of the Roman Empire came the Christians, who helped undermine the Roman Empire and grew to be one of the dominant world religions.

Christianity gained a foothold in Rome and Constantinople. The struggle for economic control and economic power was up for grabs until Charles Martel defeated the Moors at Poitiers in 732. The Moors had moved from Africa up through Spain and threatened to take over all of Europe, since they had already conquered a large part of it. Western civilization might not have existed without the victory of Charlemagne. "It was through him that the Atlantic World established contact with the ancient cultures of the Mediterranean world."[2] When Charlemagne visited Rome in the year 800 the Pope crowned him Emperor of a new Holy Roman Empire, which gave the Pope supremacy over the Emperor.[3] This act served to establish a contact with Rome and dominance of Christian religion over Europe, for at that time most Christians were Catholic. Architecture, mosaic murals, and book illumination, as well as paintings and sculpture, flourished throughout the Carolingian Empire of Charlemagne.

The arts that flourished were created for the purpose of advancing the church. Styles developed and were later named or identified. The Romanesque was followed by the Gothic and influenced the Renaissance, which flowered in Italy, France, Germany, Spain, and the Low Countries of Flanders and Holland. Each country developed its unique style, distinctive in character but dedicated to the same major religious objective. The styles that emerged shaped the ethnic nature of the art produced.

Protestantism

In northern Europe, around 1500 and about the time of Columbus's voyage, seeds of religious dissent were being sown. Erasmus, a friend of Hans Holbein, and a great traveler to European capitals, questioned certain doctrines and created a stir in European capitals. Luther, following the line of thought advanced by Erasmus, wrote in German instead of Latin and translated the Bible into German, which gave people a chance not only to read Holy Writ for themselves, but also gave them the tools of thought as well.[4] The time was ripe for the spread of this translation, since the Gutenburg press had recently been invented and the protests developed into the period known as the Reformation. The Reformation changed the mood and direction of the arts. Bright and gay colors became somber and dull, lines lost their curves and no longer danced in opposing rhythmic movements but became straight. The vertical and horizontal dominated, representing piety. Control of the life and belief also became rigid, and for some, unbearable. The mood of the Reformation was clearly uppermost in the thoughts and actions of early settlers of the United States who came from Protestant countries. The pagentry and colorful ceremonies of southern European people, who came from predominantly Catholic countries, and who settled the southern sections of the United States, were in sharp contrast with the settlers in the northern parts. The sharp severity of the Puritans severely limited colors and elaborate decoration in costume and furnishings of the northern settlers. Those who came for religious freedom imposed rigid rules in the areas they controlled and were out of tune with ceremonial practices of the Indians found living there.

In time a number of different sects arrived, and although they held to similar beliefs, there were sharp differences among them. As a result, those who were not in control and not in agreement with those in control found it necessary to move to other locations where they could command. Some sought out such areas before coming to the new country.

The town of Salem, North Carolina was founded by a devout group of German people whose faith had flourished for three hundred years, tracing back to a Bohemian martyr who was burned at the stake. Religious persecution forced the members into hiding

2. Sir Kenneth Clark, *Civilization: A Personal View* (New York: Harper & Row, 1970), p. 18.
3. Ibid., p. 20.
4. Ibid., p. 160.

and in the early 1700s a few escaped from Moravia and sent missionaries to the New World.

In 1776 they started to build Salem—the word means peace—in the Carolina wilderness. Unlike other American towns, Salem was a planned community. It was operated as a congregational town; the economics as well as spiritual affairs of the people were directed by the church. . . .

These people believed "the work of their hands" as well as stirrings of their consciences was direct expression of the will of God. Thus, skilled work, frequent worship, much music, both sacred and secular, was important to them.[5]

Traders came from many miles to buy the wares of the talented Moravian craftsmen of Salem. Records reveal that George Washington spent two nights in a Salem tavern, renowned for its comfort and hospitality. Salem united with Winston in 1913, and has continued to grow, and this historic area has been under restoration since 1950. Of the original buildings, one now houses the Salem Museum where folk art of the period can be viewed and studied.

Another group, the Separatists, a sect originally from Württemberg, had suffered the French invasion led by Louis XIV, the Sun King, and subsequently the Napoleonic wars, came in search of religious freedom. Neither church nor state had offered solace to this group of dissenters, and many had been jailed because they objected to hymns and liturgy, which they thought to be too worldly. This group settled in Ohio with the aid of Quakers in Philadelphia, and they named their settlement Zoar. In a short time, under the leadership of Joseph Baumeler, houses were built, land turned, and a communal type of living established where membership was required and where the leaders were elected for a five-year period. Non-Germans were excluded from membership.

The basis for this discrimination was ostensibly the linguistic, cultural and religious differences that might have clashed if various nationalities had mingled at Zoar.[6]

The constitution provided for two classes of membership, first and second class. After a probationary period through application and interviews, one became first class upon signing the constitution of the society.

Although the economy of Zoar was based mainly on agriculture, other industry developed and flourished. Skilled craftsmen developed and helped make the community practically self-sustaining. All the foods except tea, coffee, rice, and condiments. were produced by the society.

Cloth, except cotton for women's dresses, and clothing, except men's hats, were Zoar manufacture. Houses were built on foundations of Zoar sandstone and roofed with Zoar tile. Most homes and other buildings were heated by Zoar made stoves. Furniture was made in the cabinet shops. Iron and tin kitchen utensils were made in the community foundry. Tools, plows and wagons were the product of local machine and blacksmith shops.[7]

A ceramic industry was developed from natural clay deposits. From all of these efforts came a highly skilled folk art and a community that rigidly shaped the thought and action of the community. A highly religious group, though unorthodox when compared with other Protestant communities, developed a style of living strongly reminiscent to that of the old country.

Baumeler's messages, which he gave at Sunday meetings, were believed to have been divinely inspired and neither he nor the congregation had faith in priests or preachers as these had gained their knowledge from books and schools and not from God. They did not believe Christ would return in person and that "the burden of salvation was therefore up to the individual who would be aided by God only if he made an effort to help himself."[8]

The Zoarites did not baptize or confirm and gave only perfunctory treatment to holy days. If Christmas or Easter came on days other than Sunday they were not recognized and work went on as usual. Even Sunday was not observed if work was pressing.

5. "History Flourishes In Old Salem," *Arizona Republic*, Phoenix, 7 August 1974, p. E2.

6. The Ohio Historical Society, *Zoar, An Ohio Experiment in Communalism* (Columbus: The Ohio Historical Society, 1960), p. 23.

7. Ibid., p. 31.

8. Ibid., p. 55.

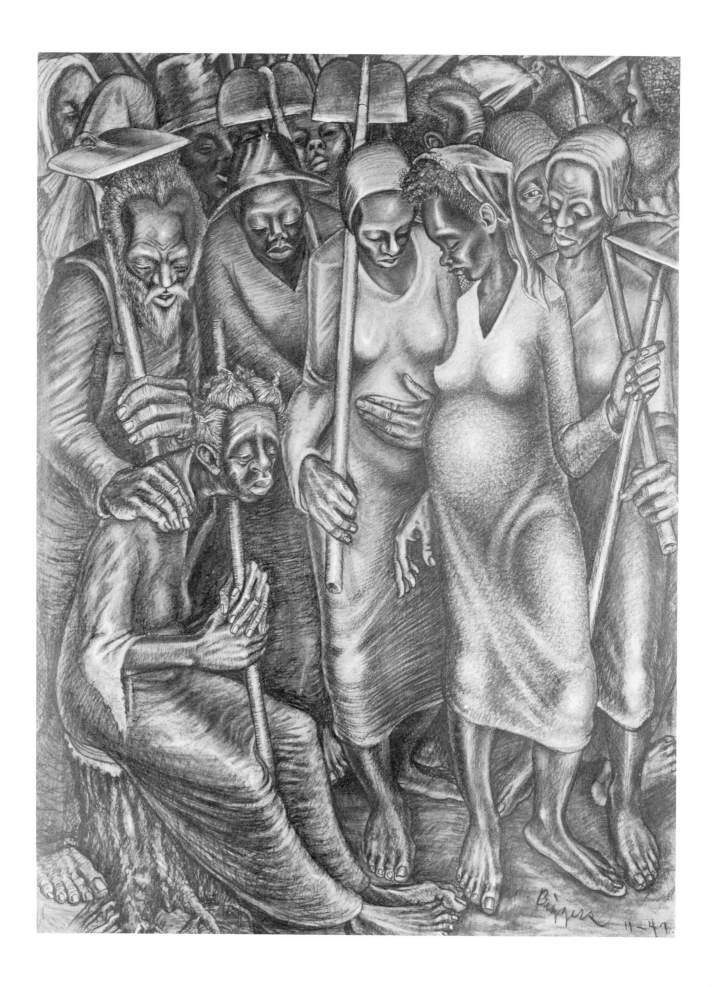

They were devoutly pacifist and did not practice proselytizing. The community prospered as long as Baumeler lived to give strong leadership, but after his death it gradually diminished and was formally dissolved at a meeting of the members on March 10, 1898.

A profile of the Shakers, another Separatist group, is given in the introduction of a catalog for an exhibition of drawings. The writer describes the Shaker as one who has

> . . . risen above physical desire and has already entered the realm of eternal life. As material values become subordinated to the spiritual, he comes into an increasing possession of "gifts" rich and ennobling. . . . There is joy in labor. He sees in the transient the image of the divine. For such ends, the Shaker explains, he separated himself from the world to obey the rule of celibacy, to purify his soul by confession, to share his earthly goods with his brethren and sisters.

The writer goes on to explain the drawings and paintings in the exhibit document,

> the aspirations towards perfection which was a profound force in Shaker life. . . . For the Shaker faith, rooted in Quakerism and Puritanism, was austere and exacting, calling for sacrifice and self-discipline.
>
> What might have been a repressive doctrine was illuminated, however, by a pervasive mysticism stemming from the "spiritual religions" of the Waldenses and other Medieval sects, from the French Prophets and English Quakers, and more immediately from the forces released by the Great Awakening in America. The Shakers reaped a goodly harvest from the revival movement of the New Light Baptists in New England and the Methodists and Presbyterians of the Kentucky and Ohio frontiers. They understood the "inner voice" of Fox, the language of Whitefield. They anticipated in their search for an ideal community, the trans-cendentalists of Brook Farm and the Fourieristic phalanges. They lived in the presence of an im-minent deity, after the pattern of the ancient Essenes and the primitive Christian church. . . .

Goodness in conduct, truthful utterance, and a sense of rightness in using materials had always been concerns of the New World Believers. They tilled the soil to "redeem" it. They made furniture for homes which were thought of as sanctuaries. The ceremonial dances, the spiritual songs . . . the messages mysteriously received from divine sources, were all phases of a deeply religious culture.[9]

These three Separatist sects, Moravians, Zoarites, and Shakers, were each Protestant but each were quite different from one another and at the same time sharply contrasted the larger, better-known religious communities of Baptist, Methodist, Presbyterian, and Lutheran, which also had their various divisions.

In general, however, Protestant religions are more alike one another than they are to the Catholic religious practices, with singular exceptions. A major difference between Protestantism and Catholicism is in the seat of power. The Catholics enjoy greater unity of dogma, more pomp and ceremony, and greater use of arts; but they are also more tightly controlled with the ultimate power resting in the hands of the Pope.

Catholicism

The decision for the Spanish to colonize the West and the Portugese the East, history tells us, was made by the Pope. After having defeated the Moors at the Battle of Cueta in 1415, the Spanish and Portugese began to vie for spheres of influence. To keep from fighting among themselves, as good Catholics should, they went to the Pope for his counsel. He told the Portugese to colonize the East and the Spanish to colonize the West.[10, 11]

In 1536 Don Antonio de Mendoza, the first viceroy of New Spain (as Mexico was known), sent Fray Marcos de Niza to follow Esteban, the Black explorer, in search of the Seven Cities of Cibola. Esteban was to locate the seven golden cities and the friar would

Figure 6.2 John Biggers. *Harvesters.* 1947. Conte crayon. Reproduced by courtesy of John Biggers.

9. Edward A. Andrews, *Shaker Inspirational Drawings* (Northampton: Smith College Museum of Art, 1960).

10. John Henrik Clarke, "Slave Revolt in the Caribbean," *Black World* 22, no. 4 (February, 1973):12-15.

11. Waldir F. Oliveira, "Consideracoes Sobre O Preconceito Racial No Brasil," *Afro-Asia* no. 8-9 (1969):7.

convert the inhabitants to the gentle creed of Christ. The viceroy could then readily obtain the gold.[12] This incident is told from many viewpoints, but all of them are essentially the same with dates varying between 1536 and 1539. The mission resulted in the death of Esteban and the return of the friar who thought he had evidence of one of the golden cities.[13] On the basis of this evidence, Coronado mounted an expedition, at the cost of a million dollars of his wife's money, in search of the gold but he returned empty-handed and a failure.

The lure of riches soon dimmed the fact that Cortez' and Coronado's mission had failed and other missions followed. The second major one was made by Juan de Onate in 1598. An impressive train of four hundred men, one hundred thirty with their families, eighty-three carts loaded with baggage, and seven thousand head of stock. They reached the pueblo of Caypa on the Rio Grande and renamed it San Juan. There a church was built and eight Franciscan missionaries were assigned to other pueblos.[14] The Indians resisted each of these colonizing thrusts but superior arms defeated them. One village was subdued after three days of fighting. The Indians surrendered with offerings of corn, blankets, and turkeys. The offerings were refused and many of the warriors were killed and thrown over the cliffs. The remaining prisoners, some seventy warriors and five hundred women and children were brought to trial and found guilty of killing eleven Spaniards and two servants. Onate sentenced all males over twenty-five years of age to have one foot cut off and to give twenty-five years of personal service; all females to give twenty years of personal service. Two Hopis captured in the fighting had their right hands cut off and were sent home as a warning. Villagra wrote an epic poem, *The History of New Mexico*, which was published in Spain in 1610. In it he celebrates the incident and tells that he transported sixty to seventy of the young captive girls to the viceroy in Mexico.[15]

In two years the Province of New Mexico was well established and Fra Benavides reported there were fifty friars, serving over sixty thousand Christianized Indians. This colonization lasted eighty years. Taxes were heavy, land was appropriated, men imprisoned and flogged for violating laws, and people were enslaved to labor for crown and church. Native worship was considered as idolatry and forty Indians,

who openly refused to give it up, were hanged.[16]

Throughout the whole period of occupation, Indian religious beliefs remained underground. On August 10, 1680, the Indians revolted, killing nearly five hundred Spaniards, including twenty-one missionaries at their altars, destroyed churches and records of church and state. "They washed all baptized Indians with amole to cleanse them of the Spanish stain."[17]

Twelve years later the Spanish again returned with a large expedition mounted by De Vargas. This time he chose kindly measures to subdue the Indians. With much diplomacy and little bloodshed, he was able to succeed in subduing the inhabitants but he found no quicksilver that he had come in search of. He renamed pueblos in honor of Catholic saints, Santa Clara, San Ildefonso, Santo Domingo, and San Juan. In each pueblo a church was built and dedicated to the saint, and the members were baptized. Missions were established throughout the southwestern United States and northern Mexico— the Franciscans along the coast of California, the Jesuits throughout lower California, and those by Father Kino throughout Sonora and southern Arizona.

The ethnic forms, brought and shaped by the Catholic priests and missionaries, are by no means limited to the southwestern part of the United States. St. Augustine, Florida, called the oldest United States city founded by Europeans was founded in early September 1565 by Pedro Mendoza de Abiles on the site of an ancient village and near where Ponce de Leon landed in 1513. The strong influence of Catholic priests must certainly have followed the conquerors in Florida as it had in New Mexico, Arizona, and California, bringing all the trappings and pageantry with it.

Louisiana, usually considered as a bastion of Catholicism in Southern United States, was possibly visited before Don Antonio de Mendoza sent Fra Marcos de Niza into Arizona in 1536. The survivors of the expedition of Cabeza de Vaca may have visited the area in 1528, and Esteban is likely to have been one of these survivors. In 1682 La Salle reached the

12. Frank Waters, *Masked Gods* (New York: Ballantine Books, 1950), p. 24.
13. Ibid., p. 27.
14. Ibid., p. 29.
15. Ibid.
16. Ibid.
17. Ibid., p. 30.

mouth of the Mississippi and claimed all of its drainage basin for France, naming the land Louisiana after Louis XIV. In 1699 Pierre Le Moyne founded the first settlement called Biloxi. In 1710 his younger brother founded Mobile. French missionaries and fur traders explored the territory, and a fort was built at Machitoches to protect the area from the Spanish. The colony was economically unprofitable, and France gave it to a merchant named Crozat. Crozat later turned it over to a company formed by John Law, who induced settlers to come in a futile "get-rich-quick" scheme.

In 1724 the *Code Noire* was adopted to completely control the lives of the great number of slaves being brought into the territory and to establish Catholicism as the state religion. Jews were barred from Louisiana under this code. Indian wars and lack of prosperity caused France to secretly secede all of the territory west of the Mississippi and the Isle of Orleans to the Spanish and to give to the British that territory east of the Mississippi. Incessant fighting persisted with continuous changes in ownership and in 1802, Spain returned Louisiana back to Napoleonic France. Evidently Napoleon didn't relish ownership of this land, for in 1803 he sold it to the United States under the presidency of Thomas Jefferson.

Catholicism had been brought to the New World by both the Spanish and the French, and Louisiana declared it a state religion. At the beginning of the nineteenth century, there was a variety of ethnic mix, such as German, Spanish, and Canary Islanders, in addition to the majority French population. Added to this mix was a huge population of African slaves and many Indian tribes. French was the official language. The ethnic mix was perhaps greater than in any other state at that time. The imprint of this ethnicity remains until this day and provides the basis for the "colorfulness" of southern Louisiana.

Religions brought to the New World by Europeans reflected centuries of development and conflict in the Old World. From Egyptian beginnings through Greece and Rome, different religions had waxed and waned, each leaving an imprint on the next. Christianity absorbed many of these features and developed new forms, each of which fomented various styles of architecture, sculpture, painting, and crafts. The course of Christianity was studded with conquest and blood as it moved north through Europe. From its Catholic origins it later split into two major opposing forces, Protestant and Catholic, and both were brought to the New World in continuing opposition to one another.

African Religions

The Europeans brought Africans to the New World by force, and these people had religions equally as potent as their captors. African religions are as ancient as man is in Africa, where his earliest remains have been found. Although there were many forms of religion in Africa, all have a basic belief in a Supreme Being, God, whom most reach in supplication through ancestors. Dr. Olfert Dapper, who visited the ancient kingdom of Benin, published in Amsterdam in 1668, one of the earliest reports on Africa. He wrote, "They well knew that a God had created the heavens and earth and was the ruler of both."[18] A generation later, another Dutchman, David van Nyendael also visited the kingdom of Benin and he wrote that

> . . . they ascribe to God the attributes of omnipotence, and invisibility . . . and believe that he governs all things by his providence. Because God is invisible they say it would be foolish to make any corporeal representations of Him, for they insist it is impossible to make an image of what one has never seen.[19]

Dr. Mungo Park, a Scotsman, explored much of the upper Niger Valley in the latter part of the eighteenth century and provided Europe with an account of that part of Africa where empires of Ghana, Melle, and Songhai had flourished in the Middle Ages. He reported that he could

> . . . pronounce without the smallest shadow of a doubt, that the belief in one God and in a future state of reward and punishment is entire and universal among them. . . .[20]

18. Leo Hansberry, "Indigenous African Religions," *Africa, Seen by American Negroes*, ed. John A. Davis (Paris: Presence Africaine, 1958), p. 85.

19. Ibid.

20. Ibid.

Figure 6.3 Romare Bearden. *The Conjure Woman*. Collage. Reproduced by courtesy of Romare Bearden.

An American missionary, the Reverend J. Leighton Wilson worked and lived for eighteen years in West Africa with peoples from the Guinea Coast to the Cameroons. He wrote a half century after Park that the

> . . . belief in some Supreme Being who made and upholds all things is universal . . . so deeply engraved upon their mental and moral nature that any system of atheism strikes them as too absurd and preposterous as to require denial.[21]

Damiao de Goes, chief historian of the kingdom of Portugal from 1546-1571, drew upon reports of travelers that the inhabitants of this part of Africa ". . . believe in one God, the creator of all things, and whom they adore and to whom they pray."[22]

Dr. Hansberry, a lifelong student of Africa, tells us that Maurice Delafosse, the ablest Africanist produced by France, published over forty works on practically all the major aspects of African life and

Figure 6.4 Dana Chandler. *Fetish #2*. Acrylic on a board, 14 x 35 inches. Reproduced by courtesy of Dana Chandler.

culture with several being devoted to African religion and related matters. Delafosse placed emphasis on the philosophical, esoteric, mystical, and metaphysical aspects rather than the ritualistic and institutionalized ones. To understand the real nature of the Negro's conception of God, the world, and humanity, one must keep in mind the important part that religious mysticism plays in both individual and group thought. He makes it clear that religious mysticism dominates the Negro's entire outlook, not only upon the mun-

21. Ibid.
22. Ibid., p. 87.

Figure 6.5 Lois Mailou Jones. *Ubi Girl from Tai Region.* 1972. Acrylic, 43¾ x 60 inches. Reproduced by courtesy of Lois Mailou Jones and from the permanent collection of the Museum of Fine Arts, Boston, Massachusetts.

Figure 6.6 Raquel Kambinda. *Omulu.* Tempera. Reproduced by courtesy of Eugene Grigsby.

dane world, but upon the supermundane world of which the visible world is but the lesser part. All individual and group activities, whether of a social, political, economic, or religious nature, are primarily determined by considerations that are essentially of a mystical and religious character. In commenting on this interesting fact he observes that the Negroes "... of whom it is sometimes said have no religion at all are in reality among the most religious people in the world."[23]

Dr. Diedrich Westerman, a German, in reference to West African beliefs wrote, "... everything owes its existence to Him, including 'all human beings who are God's children' for no human beings are earth's children."[24]

It is interesting to note that travelers, researchers, and explorers of Africa, who were serious students

of the culture and who reported their findings before the advent of the slave trade, are in agreement with students of African culture, who have been active in recent years.

Traditional western notions of African culture is at odds with these reports, which stem from literature that attempted to justify the slave trade on a moral basis for economic profit. African religions were presented as a vast disorder of senseless superstitions employing fetishes either worshipped as gods or as talismans in all kinds of dark and diabolical rites.

Hansberry tells us that these western notions originate from the fact that earlier observers, and

23. Ibid., p. 88.
24. Ibid., p. 89.

69

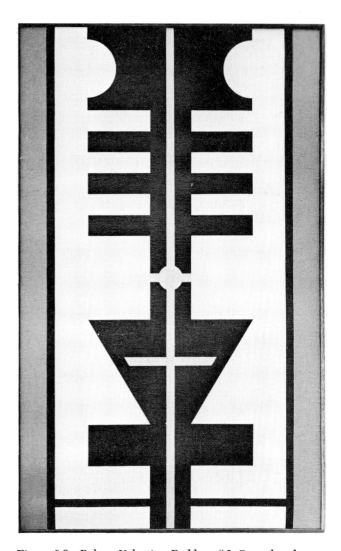

Figure 6.7 Rubem Valentim. *Emblem #1*. Reproduced by courtesy of Rubem Valentim.

Figure 6.8 Rubem Valentim. *Emblem #2*. Reproduced by courtesy of Rubem Valentim.

some recent ones, were unaware of the spiritual foundations or esoteric aspect, or the outward exoteric elements, including dogma, rites, and ceremonies were means through which allegiance to the spirit and inner teachings of the religion could be expressed.[25] He feels that the foundation for this misunderstanding was laid by Peiter de Marsees in *Description of Guinea*, which first appeared in 1604.

One hundred fifty years later Charles de Brosses, a Frenchman following de Marsees, published *Du Culte des dieux fetiches*, which presented the thesis that all religions originated in what he called "fetishism." The worship of material objects believed to embody some spiritual powers. The French philosopher Auguste Comte picked up the idea and elabo-

rated on it in his famous treatise *Philosophie positive*, which appeared between 1830 and 1842. The idea was further elaborated by the German Fredrick Waitz, then by the English ethnologist E. B. Taylor, and finally by Herbert Spencer.

By the middle of the nineteenth century, the general point of view had become so firmly fixed in western thought that few if any scholars or travelers dared to challenge it, even when evidence suggested an opposite course.[26] Any differences

25. R. P. Temples, *The Bantu Philosophy* (Paris: Presence Africaine, 1948).
26. Hansberry, "Indigenous African Religions," p. 98.

70

Figure 6.9 Rubem Valentim. *Emblematic Object #1.* Reproduced by courtesy of Rubem Valentim.

Figure 6.11 Rubem Valentim. *Emblem #3.* Reproduced by courtesy of Rubem Valentim.

Figure 6.10 Rubem Valentim. *Emblem #5.* Painting with a Shango double ax symbol. Reproduced by courtesy of Rubem Valentim.

Figure 6.12 Rubem Valentim. *Emblem #5.* Reproduced by courtesy of Rubem Valentim.

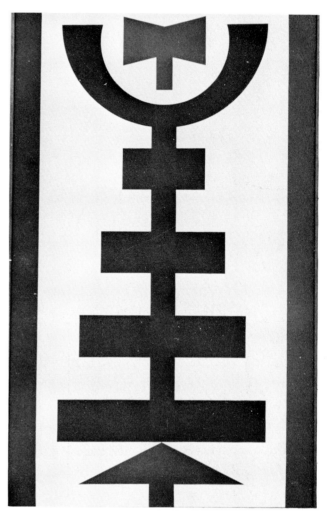

Figure 6.13 Rubem Valentim. *Emblem #4.* Reproduced by courtesy of Rubem Valentim.

were ascribed to outside influences. Wooden figurines and other objects, which the Portugese called *fetico* and the Dutch *fetisso* (roughly meaning "made fake" or "false god") and which were used much as some Christians use beads and the crucifix in religious ceremonies, were mistaken by early observers as African gods. . . .[27]

Hansberry sums up his paper with the following comment.

Recent reappraisals of indigenous African religions make it clear that many of the so-called pagan peoples of the continent are now, and have been firmly convinced, that God does exist and is eternally just, that there is purpose and meaning in life. . . .[28]

Although the Africans believe in a Supreme Being, the fact has been obscured due to the many variations used by different people, the different and elaborate ceremonies, and a pantheon of lesser deities in

supplication to the deity. Cosmogonies of African religion emphasize the train of deities as former ancestors, and many cults dedicated to various deities intercede for the supplicant. Slaves brought to the New World were at times able to continue practicing religion in the same manner as they had in Africa, but most often the practice of such religion was forbidden. There is some indication that not all Africans who came to the New World were slaves, and that some may even have come before Columbus.

Floyd W. Hayes cites references of the presence of Africans in America before the coming of Columbus.[29]

27. Ibid., p. 97.
28. Ibid., p. 99.
29. Floyd W. Hayes, "The African Presence in America Before Columbus," *Black World* 22, no. 9 (July 1973):4-11.

Figure 6.14 Rubem Valentim. *Emblem #6*. Reproduced by courtesy of Rubem Valentim.

Figure 6.15 Rubem Valentim. *Emblematic Object #2*. Reproduced by courtesy of Rubem Valentim.

Researchers support this thesis based on evidence from language, customs, food, religion, crops, and artifacts in addition to records. Abubakari II, a follower of Islam, who was curious about the Arab thesis that the world was round instead of flat, sent a fleet of four-hundred ships into the Atlantic, instructing his captains not to return until land was found or supplies exhausted. When only one ship returned, Abubakari formed another fleet and took charge of two thousand ships in search of land across the Atlantic.

The religion of the Yoruba of west Africa is an example of African religions. The Yoruba occupy considerable territory that covers southwest Nigeria and adjacent areas of Dahomey (now named Benin) and Togo. Contradictory versions exist of the Yoruba tradition of origin but there seems to be general agreement that Oduduwa was the first king (also called Oba, Oni, Obatala). Tradition varies as to whether he descended from the sky or immigrated from outside of Yorubaland. He is related to the founding of Ile Ife, the first location of the Yoruba and his sons founded other kingdoms. Ultimately, Oduduwa and his immediate descendents were worshipped as Orishas or gods.[30]

30. R. C. C. Law, "The Heritage of Oduduwa: Traditional History and Political Propaganda Among the Yoruba." *Journal of African History*, vol. 2, no. 14 (1973): 208-211.

Figure 6.16 Micumba, food left for the gods (Yoruba) in Rio de Janeiro, Brazil. Reproduced courtesy of the author.

A number of cults headed by Orishas are known among the Yoruba. Carroll emphasizes, however, that

> . . . Yoruba people believe in a supreme spirit who is remote from the affairs of men; he receives little or no liturgical worship; in between God and man is a host of spirits who influence human affairs, benevolently or otherwise; there are also the ancestors who represent the continuity of the family and guard its conduct and survivals.[31]

Dr. Baloji Idowu rejected this outline of Yoruba belief and claims that ". . . for the Yoruba, God is not remote but imminent, and in spite of the absence of liturgical worship they constantly refer to God and pray to him.[32] At any rate, it is clear that the spirits between God and man have been symbolically represented in sculpture and design. Striking examples of these Yoruba deities exist in the New World, particularly in South America and to a lesser degree in the United States. Dr. S. I. Biobaku, Director of the Yoruba Historical Research Scheme, expressed gratitude for a booklet written by Joan Wescott on Yoruba art in German and Swiss museums. In this booklet, Wescott commented on the Orishas who gave rise to the art objects and in whose worship they function. This list includes:

The Ogboni Society, a secret society of elders whose ritual includes an ancient form of earth worship. The art style of the Ogboni is the most abstract and sophisticated of the Yoruba cults, and they employ brass or bronze for all except elaborately carved wooden drums.

Ifa is an oracle of divination where men learn how to relate to the cult. Ritual objects are highly decorated and include boards, bowls, and ivory or wood *iroke*. The *iroke* is tapped or shaken to invoke the god, the bowls contain the divining palm nuts, the board is spread with flour or sand in which the results of divination are inscribed.

The Ogungun Society combines ancestor worship with political functions. They make masks that reflect their ancestors' concerns with all aspects of life. These masks are expressive and range from solemn to grotesque and satirical.

The Orishafunfun are described as being among a group of "white gods" associated with creation and includes Obatala and many gods of localities.

The Ibeji are protectors of twins, a special gift from the gods. An image is carved when a twin dies, and this is cared for by the surviving twin or its mother.

Eshu or *Elegbara* is the mischief maker and the messenger of the gods. He also inhabits the crossroads and marketplaces and is the guardian at doorways.

Gelede is a masked society of men who dance to please women, to promote fertility, and to prevent witchcraft.

Shango is god of thunder and lightning and also god of iron. Shango is represented by a double ax symbol.[33]

Other cults have special implements, figures, ceremonial stools, and bowls, required for the payment of homage to the god of the cult. These include *Osumare*, the rainbow-serpent, and *Omolu*, the god of smallpox.

In Brazil, ceremonies known as "Micumba" and "Candomblé" parallel the religious practices of the Yoruba and use the same Orishas. Sometimes the meaning of the god seems to have undergone a change, but most remain exactly the same. In Sao

31. Keven Carroll. *Yoruba Religious Carving: Pagan and Christian Sculpture in Nigeria and Dahomey* (New York: Praeger, 1967), p. 39.

32. Ibid.

33. Joan Wescott, *Yoruba Art, in German & Swiss Museums* (Ibadan: Yoruba Historical Research Scheme, 1958).

Paolo I was given a painting representing *Omolu,* by the artist Raquel Kambinda. On the reverse side of the painting was written, "Omulu, god of health" rather than smallpox.

In Rio de Janeiro, the deity Yemanja, another Orisha, is celebrated at the end of each year. On Copacabana Beach thousands of devotees and well-wishers send paper boats out to sea filled with food and gifts for this deity.

Salvador has one of the largest populations of Black people in Brazil and among some of its inhabitants, Yoruba is still spoken. The bank of Bahia's major branch in the capital city of Salvador has on its walls twenty-seven wooden panels, carved in bas-relief, representing different Orishas with the symbolic dress, animal, and implements related to the god or goddess of the particular panel. Decorative elements, cowrie shells, beads, metal, and other materials heighten the aesthetic effect of the carvings. This amazing series of panels was created by the Brazilian artist, Carybé, who himself is an *Oba* in a Candomblé of Salvador. He is also the creator of two murals in the American Airlines Terminal building at Kennedy Airport in New York City, which may include symbolic Candomblé representations.

Rubem Valentim, another outstanding Brazilian artist, and also an *Oba* of a Candomblé uses symbols of the Yoruba Orishas in his paintings. Valentim paints in the hard-edge manner using flat colors and contrasting patterns which are juxtaposed one against another, creating a variety of visual tensions. The double ax symbol of Shango is quite prominent in most of Valentim's works which have been exhibited internationally.

I witnessed a Candomblé ceremony that took place on the outskirts of Salvador and was one of four persons in the crowded room who were not members of the Candomblé. Unlike the performances staged for tourists within the city, this one was for members only. Many of the elements of the Candomblé I had read about were seen firsthand. The orchestra of drummers kept up a rhythmic pattern of sound throughout the evening. The high priestess, to whom each of the officials, all of the participants and many of those in the audience paid special homage, set the stage for the actions that followed. With the exception of one, all the dancers were women. They moved in measured steps and rhythmic cadence in a counterclockwise direction. In turn, each dancer

was possessed by the Orisha to whom he or she was devoted and, when possessed, went into a trance. During the trance the devotees danced solo, sometimes in a tranquil manner and sometimes in a violent manner, until the spirit subsided. Some had to be entranced by their Orisha, they retired to a special house and changed into the costume of their Orisha. and changed into the costume of their Orisha.

After a long "intermission" the dancers returned, splendidly dressed in the costume of the Orisha and holding the implement associated with the particular god or goddess. The male dancer carried the knife of Shango and danced superbly, although at times he threatened and brandished the knife. The high priestess held off the entranced dancers, whenever they came too close, with a special rattler. We were instructed to hold up our hands, palms outstretched, and the vibrations of our being would ward off any malevolence. This experience dramatically displayed the strong influence of Yoruba tradition, which is still practiced in Brazil.

Islam

The influence of Islam on the American continent, although not as obvious as other religions brought from Europe and Africa, must not be minimized as nonexistent. Much Islamic influence is buried in that of the Spanish, African, or Near East, but on close observation there is significant cultural influence to be found. Perhaps the most recent and most vocal outcropping is found in the "Black Muslim" movement of the United States. In other parts of the world, particularly Africa, Islam is quickly gaining adherents.[34]

One hundred years after the death of Muhammed, his zealous followers conquered an empire as great as Rome at its zenith. This area extended across southwestern Europe, northern Africa, and all of Arabia. It also included western and central Asia from India in the east and Spain in the west. Moslems assimilated into their creed, speech, and physical

34. Bernard Cushmeer, *This Is The One* (Phoenix: Truth Publications, 1970).

type more aliens than any stock before or since.[35] At one point they invaded Spain and threatened to overrun Gaul itself, making converts as they conquered.

Islam, the religion founded by the Prophet Muhammed who died in A.D. 632, has, in the course of time, become a way of life, like Judaism, rather than just a religion.[36] The general impression has been advanced that Islamic culture forbade the representation of the human form, but this is not quite true. Much has been written about Islamic antipathy toward imagery of any kind. In actuality the Koran condemns only idolatry, and the authority that prohibits art is the *Hadith*, an Islamic law which enjoys as much power and sanctity as the Koran. This austerity is undoubtedly derived from Islam's Jewish heritage, which taught that producing a representation of a living creature was to usurp the creative prerogative of God.[37]

Grube tells us that

The misconception that Islam was an iconoclastic or anti-imagistic culture and that the representation of human beings or living creatures in general was prohibited, is still deeply rooted although the existence of figurative painting in Iran has been recognized now for almost half a century. There is no prohibition against the painting of pictures or the representation of living forms in Islam, and there is no mention of it in the Koran.[38]

The Moslem conquests under the Umayyads in A.D. 661-750 extended Muhammedan control throughout Spain and to the borders of France in the west, all across northern Africa, through all of Arabia, through the middle eastern territories of Mespotamia, Iran, and Afghanistan to the western borders of India. The Moslem world of 1920 did not include Spain, but it did cover portions of Africa down to the horn of west Africa and straight across the continent to Somalia.[39] Mali, Senegal, and parts of Nigeria and Ghana had converted Muslims long before Columbus' famous voyage. Captured victims of Arab slave traders, converts to Islam, were *supposedly* absolved from being sold as slaves. In the eyes of Islam all Muslims of every race and country were equal in the face of Allah on the day of judgment.[40] The ties of Islam to the community of faith were to supercede the bonds of kinship. The inauguration of

the Islamic dispensation was to herald a new relation between men.

The white man was not to be above the black nor the black above the yellow, said the tradition, all men were to be equal before their Maker, and equal before the law. Among believers, superiority was to be marked only by priority in the faith or by stricter observance of its precepts.[41]

Islamic religion was based on five concepts: 1) there is no deity but Allah, and Muhammed is the prophet of Allah; 2) the requirement to pray five time a day; 3) to give alms to the needy; 4) to endure the thirty-day fast of Ramadan when neither food nor drink could be consumed between sunrise and sunset; 5) to make the pilgrimage to Mecca and Medina.[42]

Similarly, all phases of art were considered equal by Islamic law, architecture and metalwork, painting and pottery, sculpture and weaving. What the European considered major and minor arts were all equal in the eyes of Islam.

By the time of the great migrations to the New World, the influence of Islam had been confined to Arabia, north and west Africa, and the Near East. Spain had become Christian, although many vestiges of Islamic art survived. Perhaps the greatest carry-over of Islamic design influences came from slaves brought from Africa where Islam and pagan religions coexisted side by side. The decorative ironworks of New Orleans, Mobile, and other Southern cities may well have been inspired by Islamic followers, who continued to make patterns of floral decorations which are seen in wood carvings as well

35. Phillip K. Hitti, *The Arabs: A Short History* (Princeton: Princeton University Press, 1949), p. 1.

36. Pratapaditya Pal, "Introduction," *Islamic Art* (Los Angeles: Los Angeles County Museum of Art, 1973), p. 9.

37. Ibid.

38. Ernst J. Grube, *The World of Islam* (New York: McGraw-Hill Book Company), p. 11.

39. Hitti, *The Arabs: A Short History*, p. 3.

40. Grube, *The World of Islam*, p. 11.

41. John Ralph Willis, "The Spread of Islam," *The Horizon History of Africa* (American Heritage Publishing Co., Inc., 1971), p. 140.

42. Ibid., p. 141.

as on furniture, bannisters, and other wood products. These designs are also found in fabric designs throughout the South.

Judaism

Judaism, like Islam, is even more a way of life than it is representative of a particular aesthetic style. More than Islam, or even Christianity, the Jewish people were more widely spread geographically, since adherents to its religion and life-styles are found in most countries of the world. The immigrant of Jewish background coming to the United States was as likely, if not more so, to reflect the ethnic quality of the country of origin. Yet, underneath a nationalist patina, lay a cultural heritage that permeated life and thought and to some degree affected the art produced. Within this context there remains a deep undercurrent in the works of many artists of Jewish background, which reflects the pride and strength of their religious background which is more likely to be sensed than analyzed.

Native American Religions

All immigrants to the Americas found native peoples who practiced a well-established religion with certain art forms closely tied to the religious ceremony. Like Islam, all of the arts were considered to be of equal importance. The forms of religion varied from one part of the continent to another, but most held certain beliefs in common.

A thesis written by Jane Kolber on the culture of the Navajo, the largest remaining Indian tribe of the United States, surveyed studies dealing with Navajo religion. She tells us that the Navajo religion is not a Sunday religion, as Christianity often tends to be, but it permeates every aspect of Navajo life. The Navajo did not hesitate to borrow and adopt components from other cultures to fit their needs. It is comprised of an intricately detailed mythology. According to tradition, they originally came from a lower world, passing through four levels and emerged into the fifth, the present one. The next world is that of the spirit, and beyond it is a world where everything emerges into the cosmos. The greatest concern of the Navajo is with the present, the fifth world. The universe contains two classes of personal forces, the ordinary human beings and the holy people, who belong to the sacred world rather than the profane world. In Navajo religion, no one person has more significance than another.

The Navajo center their religious practices on the art of curing to maintain health. They value highly those skills in ceremonial arts which promote curing, such as singing, dancing, making dry-paintings, and telling stories. The native practices bring good results, often as great as those of the White man. The Navajo religion is not dying out, as often predicted, because myth and ritual tend to preserve ancient traditions which serve as brakes on the speed of cultural change. There is evidence that ceremonies are being performed more frequently than ever. Witchcraft is sometimes performed by aberrant singers for personal ends, but even this helps maintain a system of checks and balances so the ceremonial practitioners and the rich are kept from attaining too much power.

Missionaries have sought to convert the Indians ever since they first landed, with various results. A Seneca chief questioned the religion of the White man asking why there were so many opposing versions of the same religion since they came from the Book and all could read the Book. The Navajos have retained their culture over centuries without use of a written language, centers of education, or a religious head.

The Navajos have difficulty in accepting an all male God when their central deity, Changing Mother, is female. The picture of God as being all good is also incomprehensible to them.

The art of a people often reflects social and religious concerns, and this reflection is not always visually represented. Kolber reported that Crapanzano expressed a disconcerning feeling while living with the Navajo and attributed it to their organization of space. "There are no centers."[43] "And there is a fear of finishing anything."[44] Kolber cites Navajo values: "Think about things so you do everything right and

43. Jane Kolber, "An Investigation of Navajo Culture with Implications for Navajo Art Education" (Master's thesis, Arizona State University, 1974), p. 42.
44. Ibid., p. 47.

Figure 6.17 Diane O'Leary. *The Stompers*. From the collection of the Heard Museum, Phoenix, Arizona.

make pretty things."[45] "Personal excellence is a value but personal success in the white American sense is not."[46]

Values of the Navajo are but an example of similar ones held by other Indian peoples. Unfortunately, these values are often in conflict with those of teachers who are non-Indian, particularly those values dealing with completing work, competition, and rejecting personal success.

Frank Waters gives detailed descriptions of Hopi mythology of the Creation, which support those of the Navajo. He tells of the "Rock" which extended

through all the previous undergrounds and protruded above this one, the core of the universe and oriented in four directions. Each side of the "Rock" was assigned a color; black on the north, white on the east, blue on the south, and yellow-red on the west.[47] Waters relates the mythology of what occurred on each level of the underworld as man emerged. He calls the Creation myth the story of evolutionary

45. Ibid., p. 48.
46. Ibid., p. 54.
47. Waters, *Masked Gods*, p. 163.

Figure 6.18 Rip Woods. Untitled. Woodcut. Reproduced by courtesy of Rip Woods and from the collection of the author.

development as well as man's journey up through four underworlds.[48] He wrote

> that in Pueblo and Navajo mythology we are dealing not with easily comprehended, childish legends, but with a cosmographic concept as abstract, imaginatively vast and old as that of any people on earth.[49]

The studies of northwest coast Indian societies by Franz Boas and his students, support the general religious concept and mythology reported by Waters. The differences between these native peoples are reflected in the art they produced and in their lifestyles. Art of the northwest coast Indians was heroic and dramatic, reflecting the vastness of their environment: ocean, mountains, and huge cedar trees.

Works produced by these peoples are perhaps the most dramatic and spectacular of any in the Americas.

Summary

The religious component of the ethnic fabric has played a major role in shaping attitudes, thinking, and actions of creators and audience alike and continues to do so far more than most of us realize. Religions, those brought to America and those indigenous to the continent, are sharply etched in their differences, yet underlying each of these is the belief in a single creator of mankind. Although immigrants to the Americas and those they found on arrival believed in a single creator, they worshipped this creator in many different ways, which gave rise to different religions and religious practices. These religions and religious practices were often in conflict with one another and at times were a source of violence.

The Christian religions brought by Europeans became dominant through force and conversion. As the wave of conquest moved from east to west, the conquerors brought Protestant and Catholic Christianity to the new lands. The largest group, the Protestants, were from England, Germany, and Holland and brought hostile attitudes toward Catholic art (with the exception of a few paintings representing Jesus, events of his life, and his disciples). Their attitudes paralleled those of Islam's hadith, in that worship of idols or any semblance of idolatry was forbidden, whereas secular art was permitted and usually encouraged. Arts were separated from everyday living and certain forms were considered higher than others. Folk art, academic art, and international art for the marketplace were encouraged, and they flourished.

Conquerors from France, Spain, and Portugal, who settled the southern boundaries of the country from Florida to Texas, in the Southwest, West, and practically all of Latin America, were largely Catholic with religious attitudes that required graphic and plastic representation of saints and religious figures. Architecture influenced by the Catholics was also

48. Ibid., p. 175.
49. Ibid., p. 166.

79

more formal and flamboyant than that of the Protestants. The Catholics, like the Protestants, however, relegated the arts to special places and considered some arts more important than others.

Religious practices of the native Americans and of the Africans brought to the continent by force were perhaps more in tune with the Catholics than with the Protestants. Each paid homage to many deities in the supplication to the one God. Catholics could not accept these deities on the same plane as their own, called them "idols," and demanded that they be destroyed. Both Catholics and Protestant outlawed the practice of religions other than Christianity whenever they were encountered and persecuted those who resisted. Intuitively, they realized that seeds of revolt could be planted in religious practice. Toussaint L'Ouverture, the liberator of Haiti, was assumed to be a true believer until he overthrew the French, then he reverted to his native Vodun.

Could it be that seeds of protest were sown in these early days of conquest; protest that resisted the downgrading of native religions; protest against accepting the religion of the conqueror; protests that sparked from time to time but burst into flames during the turbulent 1960s?

7 Protest: A New Component of Ethnic Art

Protest is as American as apple pie. The United States was born in protest and the Boston Tea Party marks that beginning. Young colonials resented the policies of England, the "Mother Country," and expressed their resentments in a dramatic deed that has been a major subject for many of the arts. History is replete with examples of protests by dissidents or conquered peoples who were denied freedom of choice, movement, work, worship, thought, or previous life-style. Even the religious movement that broke with Catholicism is called "Protestant" after the word protest.

Protest, sometimes violent, sometimes sullen, at times overt and at other times covert, came with the first settlers and continues today. Protest became the basis—the meat and sinew, the bone and marrow—of much creative thought expressed in literature, music, dance, and the visual arts. Long before the Boston Tea Party, Indians of the Southwest violently protested the invasion of the Spanish.

Native American Protests

Coronado's first venture into the Southwest was a failure and after two years he straggled back to Mexico defeated by the Indians. Juan de Onate decided to conquer the land in 1598 and, with his retinue of soldiers, priests, and animals was able to remain for eighty years before every pueblo rebelled on August 10, 1680, driving the Spaniards from their land. Twelve years later de Vargas came, this time peacefully, in search of quicksilver only to return empty-handed. Some fifty years were to elapse before the Spanish gained a foothold, and even then they were plagued with raids by bands of Indians.

On the east coast, friendly Indians received the Pilgrims, who came in protest to religious practices in Europe. There existed among these Indians a confederacy of the United Five Nations, established nearly fifty years before the landing of the Pilgrims. The Mohawk, Seneca, Oneida, Onondaga, and Cayuga, and later the Tuscarora, had joined together to maintain peace among themselves. Authority within the structure flowed upward from elected chiefs who were confirmed by popular vote. The Onondaga did not vote, but they acted as moderator. Later the structure of the thirteen English Colonies was strikingly similar to the Five Nation structure with the exception that the Five Nations Council included women.

Friendship between the newcomers and the Indians deteriorated when the former demanded land belonging to the Indians and conformity to the religion and life-style they had brought. The English Protestants sought to impose a new pattern of life, but they refrained from social mixing and intermarrying except in isolated cases.

The Spanish Catholics destroyed the Indian culture and intermarried with the Indians to create the *mestizo*. The English Protestants destroyed both the Indian culture and the Indians themselves.[1]

1. Frank Waters, *Masked Gods Navajo and Pueblo Ceremonialism* (New York: Ballantine Books, 1950), p. 59.

"What is more, the Jesuits sought to destroy, or at least castrate, every virile expression of religious or artistic culture that was not in agreement with Catholic morality and European conventions."[2]

Indians inhabiting the Atlantic coast were pictured by the settlers, and even by such prominent persons as Ben Franklin, as savages who should be destroyed. This picture was faulty and vicious. The largest of the Iroquoian tribes, the Cherokee, invented an alphabet, wrote a constitution, established a legislature, a judiciary, and executive branch, and stopped fighting in 1794 to honor a treaty with the United States. According to the treaty they were confined to seven million acres of mountain country in Georgia, North Carolina, and Tennessee. In 1828, gold was discovered on their land and in the short time of ten years the Cherokee were deprived of these lands and forcefully moved west of the Mississippi. Of the fourteen to seventeen thousand who marched on this "Trail of Tears," some four thousand died on the way. The story of Indian tribes across the country is similar to that of the Five Nations and the Cherokee, particularly those of the eastern states. Indians of the western states were able to resist longer, particularly the Apache, Hopi, and Navajo, but they also experienced their "Trail of Tears." For the Navajo it was the Bosque Redondo.

Led by Kit Carson, the Navajo were driven into the mountains, their crops and animals destroyed, and they were kept in a near-starving condition during the cold winter until they surrendered. Eight thousand Navajo were forced to march to captivity in Bosque Redondo, 180 miles southeast of Santa Fe, with Fort Sumner as its center. In 1868, four years later, due to exorbitant costs, impossible living conditions, and controversy between the War Department and the Department of the Interior, the Navajos were set free. General Sherman, who supervised the removal, wrote that ". . . we have chosen a small part of their old country, which is as far out of the way of the whites and of our future possible wants as possible. . . ." This location, ". . . consisted of 5500 square miles of almost uninhabital desert, located in the very center of the wilderness hinterland of the United States. . . ."[3]

Indians of the United States have not forgotten their "Trails of Tears" and increasingly protest their conditions. The 1972 violence at Wounded Knee is but one example of protest, though all are not violent.

The image of the "noble savage," with all the stereotypes that go with it, was the general image that propaganda provided on the American Indian. They were supposed to be content, living in their tents and pueblos, riding their ponies bareback across the vast plains and tabletop mountains that they called home. Nineteenth- and early twentieth-century literature, music, painting, sculpture, and dance supported this image. Little, if any, of this was created by the Indians themselves.

Black Protests

A similar stereotype was applied to Black people who had been brought from Africa. Slaves were depicted as happy-go-lucky savages, lucky to have been rescued from heathen Africa where they might have been eaten, since cannabalism was supposed to be a way of life. They seldom were unhappy and, when not picking cotton, were singing and dancing. One could hardly expect such "happy people" to revolt or protest their condition. The opposite to the stereotype is closer to the truth. They were not happy with their lot and constantly rebelled. Throughout the North and the South there was constant fear of slave revolts. Herbert Aptheker reports seeing records of about two hundred fifty slave revolts and conspiracies prior to the Emancipation Proclamation.

The first slave conspiracy occurred in 1663 when White indentured servants teamed with slaves against their master in Gloucester County, Virginia. Blacks were rapidly outnumbering Whites in eastern Virginia, and repeated scares of revolt occurred in 1687, 1709, 1710, 1722, 1723, and 1730. In 1726 a patrol system was set up in Virginia in an attempt to control revolts.[4]

In 1652, the Quakers made the first protest against the institution of slavery in their colony of Warwick, and in 1688 the Mennonites of Germantown,

Figure 7.1   H. Whiteman. Untitled. From the collection of the Heard Museum, Phoenix, Arizona.

2. Gilberto Freyre, *The Masters and the Slaves* (New York: Alfred A. Knopf, 1946), p. 107.

3. Waters, *Masked Gods*, p. 72.

4. Joanne Grant, ed., *Black Protest: History, Documents and Analysis* (Greenwich: Fawcett Publications, Inc., 1968), p. 36.

Figure 7.3 Hale Woodruff. *The Amistad Mutiny Mural,* "The Mutiny Aboard the Amistad, 1839." Oil. Reproduced by courtesy of Hale Woodruff and from the collection of Talladega College, Talladega, Alabama.

Pennsylvania protested. One major difference between the African and the Indian is the fact that the Indians held lands the colonists wanted, whereas the Blacks were brought to the country and were considered as property, which had to be protected. There was a dilemma when the property got out of hand and caused the loss of other slave property or of real estate property owned by the master.

Two important slave plots, one a serious insurrection, disturbed the peace of New York City in 1712 and 1741. In revenge for ill-treatment by their masters, twenty-three Negroes rose on April 6, 1712, to slaughter the whites and killed nine before they were overwhelmed by a superior force. The retaliation showed an unusual barbarous strain on the part of the Whites. Twenty-one Negroes were executed, some were burnt, others hanged, and one broken on the wheel. In 1741, another plot was reported in New York involving both whites and blacks. . . .[5]

In 1750 Crispus Attucks escaped from his master in Framingham, Mass. Twenty years later he was the

first person killed in the Boston Massacre, the shot that brought on the American Revolution.

Throughout the South, revolts and conspiracies occurred more often than the records show. Many of these were led by religious leaders, possessed by the "spirit of Jesus," in much the same way their counterparts in Africa had become "possessed" by an Orisha. The parallels between the counterparts in Africa, South America, and the Caribbean suggest interesting research that needs to be done. The ingredients are similar—music, dance, and being possessed by a god or Orisha. In the United States some units of the ceremony, such as sculptural representation, are missing, but these seemed to have been present in spirit if not in form.

The most dramatic of the recorded conspiracies and revolts were led by such religious men as Gabriel Prosser (note the first name), Denmark Vesey, and Nat Turner.

Gabriel, a deeply religious man, laid plans for a revolt in 1800. The plan was to attack Richmond and spare only Whites who were French, Quaker, or Methodist. He was inspired by the example of Toussaint in Haiti and the emancipation of the Israelites

Figure 7.2 Dale Davis. *Relief Sculpture.* Reproduced by courtesy of Brockman Gallery Productions, Inc.

5. Ibid.

Figure 7.4 Jacob Lawrence. *John Brown, John Brown Series*. 1941. Gouache on paper, 20 x 14 inches. Reproduced by courtesy of Jacob Lawrence and from the collection of The Detroit Institute of Arts.

from Egypt, and he encouraged some eleven hundred slaves to follow him.

Numerous slave plots occurred in South Carolina but most of these appear to have been abortive. The greatest threat was created by Denmark Vesey in 1822. Vesey was a free Negro living in Charleston where he had come from his native home of St. Thomas V.I., West Indies. There, Vesey had purchased his freedom from lottery prize money and at the time he worked as a carpenter. Vesey was also inspired by the example of Toussaint and swore to

win the freedom of other Black people. He preached of the intolerable conditions under which they lived. A White man was to purchase the guns for the revolt, but it was a "faithful slave" who exposed the plot, as it was in the case of Gabriel.[6] It took patience and perseverance as Vesey slowly accumulated money and property to institute his plot. For five years he worked, preached, and quoted from Toussaint and the Bible, telling how the "Children of Israel" had been freed from bondage. Like the Zoarites, he admonished, "God only helps those who help themselves."[7]

Nat Turner was more successful in revolt. Called the Prophet, he was feared and respected by Black and White alike. He immersed himself in religion, saw visions and heard voices, as he carefully gathered recruits for the fateful day of August 31, 1831. Grant feels that contemporary accounts tend to overemphasize his leanings toward mysticism and understate the background of unrest.[8] Mystic or not, the trail of terror left by Nat Turner and his followers caused a frenzy of fear among plantation owners. Throughout that terrible night no one with a White skin was spared except a family of poor Whites who owned no slaves. Women, children, and men fled to the swamps or flocked to public buildings and barricaded doors. Some left the country, others left the state.

The following day Turner's army routed one group of Whites advancing on his troops, but the Whites were later reinforced with a larger group who put the slaves to rout. Nat eluded capture for almost two months, and while he was at large, panic seized large parts of Virginia, North Carolina, and Maryland. False rumors abounded, and Nat was reportedly seen in several areas at the same time. He was finally captured in October and was hanged on November 11, 1831. Nat prophesied that it would grow dark and rain after his execution. It did actually rain, and for some time after there was a dry spell which alarmed Whites as well as Blacks.[9] Bennett claims that the impact made by Nat Turner on the antebellum South was as great as that of John C. Calhoun or Jefferson Davis.[10]

6. Ibid., p. 42.
7. Lerone Bennett, Jr., *Before the Mayflower* (Chicago: Johnson Publishing Company, 1961), p. 115.
8. Grant, *Black Protest*, p. 40.
9. Bennett, *Before the Mayflower*, p. 125.
10. Ibid., p. 118.

Figure 7.5 Charles White. *General Moses*. Conté crayon. Reproduced by courtesy of and from the collection of Golden State Mutual Life Insurance Company.

A celebrated revolt took place on the slaving ship *Amistad*. Before the ship reached the American shore, slaves overpowered the captain and took charge. They ordered the captain to return to Africa, but unfortunately they were not navigators and did not realize until it was too late that the ship had sailed into Boston harbor, where the slaves were captured and jailed. Joseph Cinqué was the leader of the revolt and was so impressive a figure that John Quincy Adams, former United States president, agreed to defend him. The defense was successful, and after the trial Cinqué and his people were permitted to return to their homeland.

Perhaps the best-known revolt against slavery was led by John Brown, a White man, who hated the institution of slavery and vowed to eliminate it. He, too, was a religious fanatic and his raid on Harper's Ferry is deeply etched in United States history. Brown and his followers, thirteen White and five Black, unsuccessfully attacked Harper's Ferry arsenal for arms and ammunition. They were defeated and

Brown was hanged at Charleston, Virginia, on December 2, 1859.

Black women played major roles in protest and revolt. Sojourner Truth and Harriet Tubman are two of the best known. Both were fanatically religious but they expressed their religion in different ways. John Brown spoke of "talking abolitionists." Bennett describes Sojourner Truth as a "talking abolitionist." A preacher, seer, and teacher, she was born Isabella, a slave, around 1797. She inherited a deep mysticism from her mother, Mau Mau Bett. At at early age she was sold and had a succession of masters. One family taught her to curse, smoke, and to be coarse and profane. For another master she had five children. After being emancipated in New York she joined a group of eccentrics who preached a religious doctrine of matched spirits and became involved in a scandal. One day in 1843, she walked out of New York City with a bag of clothes, twenty-five cents, and a new name, Sojourner Truth.

Figure 7.6   Charles Alston. *America, America*. Oil. Reproduced by courtesy of Charles Alston.

Figure 7.7 Pablo Picasso. *Guernica*. 1937, May-early June. Oil on canvas, 11 feet 5½ inches x 25 feet 5¾ inches. On extended loan to The Museum of Modern Art, New York, from the artist. Reproduced by courtesy of The Museum of Modern Art.

From that date she walked the land, preaching, teaching, lecturing. The great and near great sang her praises and quoted her strong, striking utterances . . . Once, at a religious meeting, a speaker praised the U.S. Constitution. Sojourner stood up, all six feet of her, and dropped her sunbonnet on the platform. "Children," she said, "I talks to God and God talks to me. I goes out and talks to God in de fields and de woods. Dis morning I was walking out, and I get over de fence. I saw de wheat a'holding up its head, looking very big. I goes up and takes holt of it. You believe it, dere was *no* wheat dere. I says, 'God, what *is* the matter wid *dis* wheat?' and he says to me, "Sojourner, dere is a little weasel [weevil] in it.' Now I hears talking bout de Constitution. It looks *mighty big*, and I feels for *my* rights, but dere ain't any dere. Den I says, 'God what *ails* dis Constitution?' He says to me, 'Sojourner, dere is a little *weasel* in it.' "[11]

Harriet Tubman, called General Moses, was an "acting abolitionist" who escaped slavery when she was about twenty-five. Not satisfied with her own freedom, she returned to the South nineteen times and brought out more than three hundred slaves. Rewards for her capture reached $40,000.

Figure 7.8 Dana Chandler. *Noddin Our Liberation Away*. 1973. Magic marker on board, 20 x 30 inches. Reproduced by courtesy of Dana Chandler.

11. Ibid., p. 145.

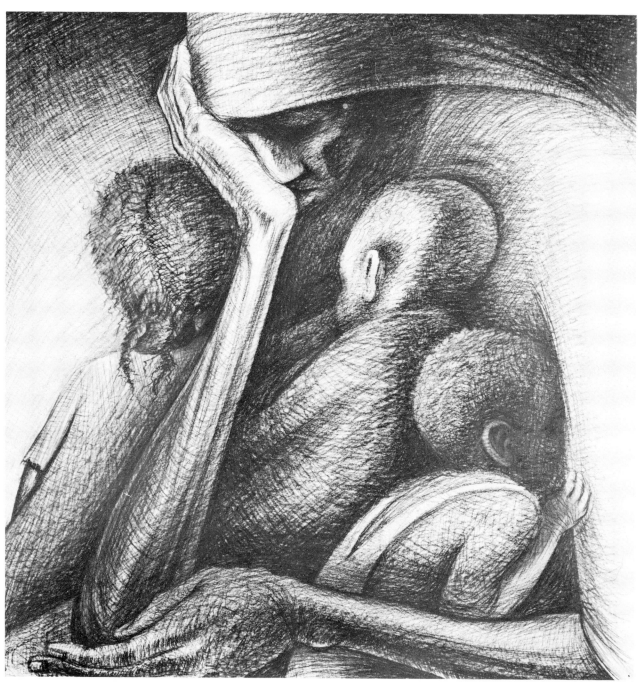

Figure 7.9   John Biggers. *The Cradle*. Carbon drawing, 22 3/8 x 21½ inches. Reproduced by courtesy of John Biggers and from the collection of the Museum of Fine Arts, Houston. Museum purchase prize, 25th Houston Artists Show, 1950.

Protest through the Arts

The arts have been a poignant means of expressing protest against inhuman conditions, and their use for this purpose has increased. The artist using protest as subject matter and as communication faces a

difficult task, for often these works degenerate into propaganda. Most works of protest are at opposite poles to the "art for art's sake" products whose reason for existence is the inherent aesthetic quality of the works themselves. Nevertheless, there have been a succession of successful artworks that have lived

Figure 7.10 Dana Chandler. *The Brother's Ready.* Acrylic on board. Reproduced by courtesy of Dana Chandler.

because of their intrinsic value long after the reason for the message of protest has gone.

The artist producing a work of protest is seldom a part of the ruling establishment against which the protest is made. Perhaps the safest and most easily executed works of protest are historical ones, which depict an event of the past; the most difficult are those which defy ruling establishments.

The majority of artworks dealing with protest appear to stem from Europe and were particularly effective during the nineteenth and twentieth centuries. Literature seems particularly well adapted to protest, and the writings of Martin Luther are among the benchmarks of protest contributing to the Protestant Reformation. Gerhart Hauptmann's play, *The Weavers,* written in 1892, was a protest against working conditions in Germany, as were the biting graphic works of Kathe Kollwitz. Francisco Goya's painting, *The Third of May,* and his etchings, *Los Caprichos,* are monuments of protest. Honoré Daumier advanced a new medium, lithography, in which his sharp barbs at segments of society landed him in jail more than once. Hogarth's etchings were an expose of social conditions in England.

The Mexican school of painting, headed by Orozco

and Rivera, was born out of protest and an attempt to bring art to the common people. Siqueiros, a third member of this movement, was even more political in his art which was of violent social protest. The works by Tamayo appear to carry on the idea of some form of protest even though he denies this to be their intent and decries the use of propaganda in art. The Mexican school of the early twentieth century became one of the most powerful art movements in the Western Hemisphere, and the basis for this school was protest.

Picasso's *Guernica* is one of the most famous examples of protest in art. This famous painting depicts the bombing of the Basque town of Guernica by the Nazis, allies of General Francisco Franco, during the Spanish civil war. Picasso was rabidly loyal to his Basque upbringing. He expresses in the mural his monumental strength as an artist without diminishing the message or the art. A recent work of protest is found in *The Gulag Archipelago* by the Russian author Solzhenitsyn, who was awarded a Nobel Prize for this book. The author chose exile from his country to express his opposition to the established order.

These are but a few examples of protest in art.

91

They deal mainly with 1) exposure of inhuman social conditions, 2) a creative reaction to repression or social ills, 3) representation of an historical act of protest, 4) celebration of heroic figures, historical or contemporary, who led or were the cause of major protests, and 5) works that incite riots and revolts. Needless to say, such subject matter deals more with social action than with art, yet in the hands of a master, the subject of protest tends to magnify the aesthetic as well as the social effect of the work. Rodin's *Burghers of Calais* would be included in this classification.

Limitations of Protest Art

The stronger and longer-lasting works of protest are those which strike a universal note to which all people can relate. Yet each one begins with pointing to a problem of a specific group of people within a limited geographical area. Because the purpose of protest is to inform rather than to entertain, to propagandize as well as to illuminate, the number of works dealing with protest is relatively small. Most artists are concerned with producing an object that has its own intrinsic value rather than one that will serve as the medium for a message. Then too, the work of protest is seldom one that is easily sold. The creator produces out of involvement in a cause rather than for business purposes. Rivera's Rockefeller Center mural was destroyed after it was completed and the artist paid, but he was not invited to return.

Little protest was noted in the visual arts during the early years of United States development. Neither folk art nor academic art were much concerned with social conditions. An occasional poster, editorial, or obscure work might express protest to some event, act, or condition, but these are rare. The great majority of these artists were tranquil practitioners, who were content to make a respectable living with their craft. One notable example, produced around 1830, is an engraving by Patrick Reason, a Black artist, of a slave in chains titled, *Am I Not Man and Brother?*

In retrospect it seems incredible that amidst all the turmoil before and after the Civil War that few sculptors or painters used their arts to protest against such social conditions; the treatment afforded the Indians in massacres; forcible removal from ancient lands to barren locations and the period when Africans

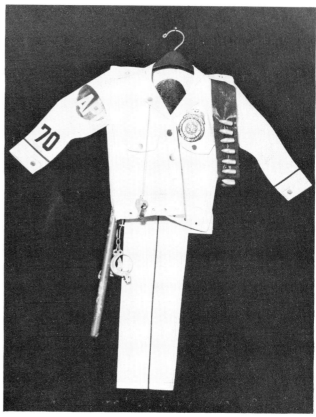

Figure 7.11 John Outterbridge. *Blow It,* from *Rag Man Series.* 1970. Painting. Reproduced by courtesy of Brockman Gallery Productions, Inc.

were brought in chains and forced to labor without wages. Artists of other countries, such as Goya, Daumier, Hogarth, Kollwitz, or the playwrights, Hauptmann and Gorky, used their art to protest social conditions. Perhaps the reason for this complacency lies in the fact that most artists were not themselves affected by these conditions, and it would take someone from an affected community to cry out in protest. This may be the reason that the engraving by Patrick Reason is among the few examples of the nineteenth century and why it was not until the twentieth century and the civil rights movement that the visual arts were used as a weapon of protest by Blacks.

Protest in Music and Literature

Few examples of protest are found in the visual arts, but many are present in music and literature, particu-

Figure 7.12 John Outterbridge. *Shopping Bag*, from *Shopping Bag Society*. 1970. Painting. Reproduced by courtesy of Brockman Gallery Productions, Inc.

larly in works created by Blacks. Music and folktales provide the most potent protest art of the times. Spirituals, folktales, and later blues throb with protest. Orators, poets, dramatists, and novelists chronicled the conditions faced by their people, past and present. Slave conspiracies, revolts and heroic figures, born in protest, were celebrated.

The Harlem Renaissance was sparked by such poets as Claude McKay, who wrote defiantly,

> If we must die, let it not be like hogs
> Hunted and penned in an inglorious spot,
> While round us bark the mad and hungry dogs,
> Making their mock at our accursed lot.
> If we must die, O let us nobly die,
> So that our precious blood may not be shed
> in vain; then even the monsters we defy
> Shall be constrained to honor us though dead!
> O Kinsmen, we must meet the common foe!
> Though far outnumbered let us show us brave,

and for their thousand blows deal one deathblow!
What though before us lies the open grave?
Like men we'll face the murderous, cowardly pack,
Pressed to the wall, dying, but fighting back![12]

Countee Cullen speaks of his bewilderment as a young Black child.

> Once riding in Old Baltimore,
>   Heart-filled, head filled with glee,
> I saw a Baltimorean
>   Keep looking straight at me.
> Now I was eight and very small,
>   And he was no whit bigger,
> And so I smiled, but he poked out
>   His tongue and called me "Nigger."
> I saw the whole of Baltimore
>   From May until December;
> Of all the things that happened there
>   That's all I remember.[13]

Melvin Tolson wrote a long poem *Dark Symphony*, which began

> Black Crispus Attucks taught
>   Us how to die
> Before white Patrick Henry's bugle breath
> Uttered the vertical
>   Transmitting cry
> "Yea, give me liberty, or give me death."

In the fourth part, *Tempo Primo*, he wrote,

> The New Negro strides upon the continent
> In seven league boots . . .
> The New Negro
> Who sprang from the vigor-stout loins
> Of Nat Turner, gallows-martyr for Freedom,
> of Joseph Cinqué, Black Moses of the Amistad
>   Mutiny,
> Of Frederick Douglass, oracle of the Catholic Man,

12. "If We Must Die," p. 36, from *Selected Poems of Claude McKay*; copyright 1953 by Twayne Publishers Inc., and reprinted by permission of Twayne Publishers, A Division of G. K. Hall & Co.
13. "Incident" from *On These I Stand* by Countee Cullen. Copyright 1925 by Harper & Row, Publishers, Inc.; renewed 1953 by Ida M. Cullen. Reprinted by permission of Harper & Row Publishers, Inc.

Figure 7.13 John Biggers. *Two Heads*. 1952. Lithograph. Reproduced by courtesy of John Biggers and from
the collection of Eugene Grigsby.

Of Sojourner Truth, eye and ear of Lincoln's
legions,
Of Harriet Tubman, St. Bernard of the
Underground Railroad.[14]

Protest in Visual Arts

Artists picked up the torch of the poets and began by
depicting heroes of these events during the waning
period of the Harlem Renaissance period and gradually increased the protest to the strong outcries

seen in the late 1960s and early 1970s. Jacob Lawrence was one of the first of these and produced a
series of egg tempera paintings on the lives of such
persons as Harriet Tubman and John Brown. Hale
Woodruff created his Amistad mural for Talladega
College. James Porter, in *Modern Negro Art* asks,

Where in all America can one find a more remark-
able group of black and white faces than in the

14. From *Dark Symphony* reprinted by permission of Arthur
Tolson.

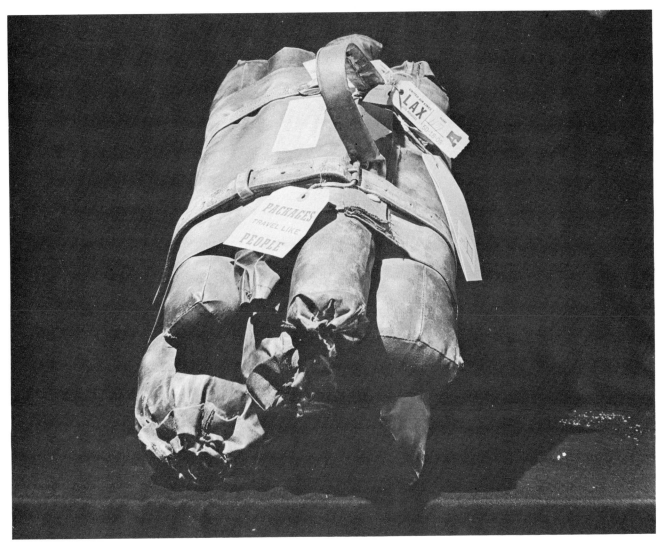

Figure 7.14 John Outterbridge. *Case in Point,* from *Shopping Bag Society.* 1970. Painting. Reproduced by courtesy of Brockman Gallery Productions, Inc.

second panel of this series, showing the slaves on trial. . . . Apart from the thorough research that the artist has expended on the costumes of the figures, there is also a variety of posture, gesture, facial expression, and grouping that builds the "psychological motif" or the dramatic tension of the whole. It must be conceded that not only does Woodruff exhibit here a fine sense of design, but also shows himself gifted in the retrospective imagination that is as indispensable to the great mural artists as to the historian.[15]

Earlier, in comparing paintings of Negro life by

Woodruff with those of Howard Cook and Thomas Benton, Porter writes . . . "the difference is great, and is in direct ratio to the artist's understanding of his material."[16]

Prior to his painting of the Amistad mural, Woodruff had spent a summer painting and studying with Diego Rivera, the Mexican master of protest painting. His early art training had been at the John Herron Art Institute, and he later received a Harmon

15. James A. Porter, *Modern Negro Art* (New York: Dryden Press, 1943), p. 121.

16. Ibid., p. 119.

Foundation award which allowed him to study in Paris at several academies and with Henry O. Tanner, the American Black artist who lived in exile in France. W.E.B. DuBois had complained that Tanner had not contributed to the American Black cause, but had become a Frenchman who painted religious scenes. Jacob Lawrence began his first series of paintings of John Brown and Harriet Tubman shortly after he had terminated his studies at the American Artists School in New York City. Both Woodruff and Lawrence were well grounded in the aesthetics of painting, as Rivera had been with his studies in Paris, before the element of protest entered their art. I doubt that either would consider their works to be protest as such, but through them, they, along with a number of unnamed artists of the same period, served to bridge a gap with younger artists who have become increasingly more outspoken in their works. Some artists have described this as the "Black Experience" in America, or the depicting of the Black experience. It takes many forms, but the basic form is protest against the conditions they experienced.

Some Results of Protest

Protest and revolt by Black people began the first day the slaves were captured and brought to America, and continues today against inhuman conditions that prevent self-realization and self-conceptualization. Not all of these protests were physical or verbal, and many took form in the arts.

Slaveholders were apprehensive of art forms and in many places outlawed dancing, beating of drums, and learning to read and write, but they seldom prohibited singing. Dancing was sometimes a signal for revolt, and those who learned to write sent letters to abolitionist papers. Frederick Douglass is one slave who learned to read and write and who later became a great orator. Oratory is considered an art form in Africa.

Carving figures, except dolls and floral decorations, was in the class of "religious idols" and was prohibited. "Slaves were forbidden to gather even for religious services except in the presence of a white person; they were forbidden to have Negro preachers."[17] Plantation owners did not realize that spirituals sung by slaves, which did not seem to appear on the list of prohibitions, were often a call for a secret meeting or a signal for some action. "My God He Calls Me,/ He Calls Me By The Thunder/ He Calls Me By Lightning/," and "Steal Away/Steal Away/ Steal Away to Jesus," this spiritual suggests visions of Shango, Yoruba god of lightning, fire, and war. These beautiful songs, based on the rhythm, melody, and chant of native African music, are embroidered with religious teachings of America, and express the slave experience that is rooted in protest to that condition. They are among the creative contributions to music that the United States has made.

Slave outbreaks were made even more ominous because slaves were often joined by Indians and at times by dissident Whites. It seemed that southerners were constantly plagued by revolts or rumors of revolt. After the Vesey uprising, because of the number of free Blacks involved, the South Carolina legislature passed an act preventing free Negroes from entering the state. The purchase of slaves from the West Indies, Mexico, South America, Europe, and the states north of Maryland were also prohibited. Slaves who had resided in these forbidden areas were likewise denied entrance into South Carolina.[18]

In 1818, Andrew Jackson defeated a force of Indians and Blacks at the battle of Suwanee, ending the first Seminole war, called by Jackson the savage and Negro war. At the Battle of Okeechobee, John Horse, a Black chief, shared command responsibilities with Seminole's Alligator Sam Jones and Wild Cat.[19]

Frank Waters tells the story of another kind of protest, subterfuge, practiced by Indians in Michoacan, Mexico. A remote church in the mountains had for years been noted for the devout attention it received. Indians from miles around came over difficult trails to kneel at its altar and bank it with flowers, as well as to listen to the young priest. This devotion for such ignorant and obstinate Indians was baffling, until a slight earthquake overturned the altar, revealing a squat stone Aztec idol.

17. Grant, *Black Protest*, p. 21.
18. Ibid., p. 42.
19. Bennett, *Before the Mayflower*, p. 367, 369.

Figure 7.15   Elizabeth Catlett. *Malcolm X Speaks for Us.*
Linocut. Reproduced by courtesy of Brockman Gallery
Productions, Inc.

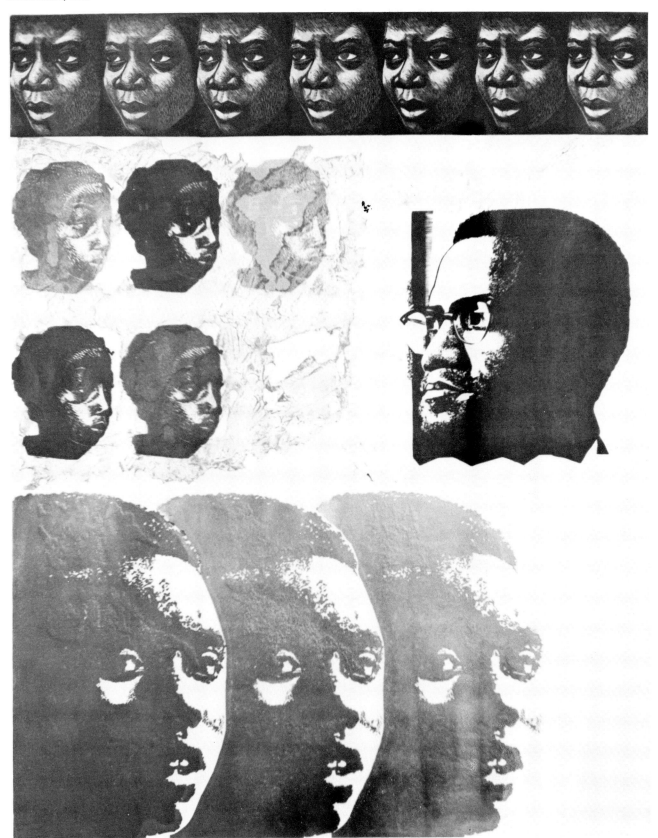

Figure 7.16 Elizabeth Catlett. *Black Woman Speaks.*
Tropical wood. Reproduced by courtesy of Brockman
Gallery Productions, Inc.

It was achieved, not surprisingly, in the name of Guadalupe, Dark Madonna of the Tepeyac, ancient Aztec mother of the gods. . . . Here occurred the "Miracle of the Roses" and here was built a church and Our Lady of Guadalupe was proclaimed the patroness and protectoress of New Spain.[20]

Negritude

Language differences between captured slaves both created a barrier and served to develop an ethnic art and new means of communication. Slaves from different language centers were put together to reduce the danger of conspiracies. The results were at first effective but later a patois developed which enabled not only slaves of the United States to communicate among themselves but with those of the Caribbean and South America as well. Leon Damas, philosopher and poet, speaks of this in tracing the development of *Negritude,* the French expression of "Black pride" of which he was a leader.

First, the black race became aware of itself through exasperation and pain. Little by little a collective sense of race was formed, with the common contrasts like ancestral level, racial persecution, and identical "mentality." But missing was the essential vector of thought which is language. Africans and West Indians have different languages, complicated by countless dialects and lack of a stable, written literature. Thus, French, like English for some, and Portugese or Spanish for others, offered itself as an excellent means for Negro expression. Like English, Portugese, and Spanish, French made it possible for all blacks to communicate with some words and identifiable symbols. It made possible a permanent correspondence between Negroes in the West Indies and those of Africa and Madagascar. . . . From 1921, thoughts and hopes of all French speaking Negroes came to cross one another and prepare the Negritude movement.[21]

This consciousness, he declares, was not racist for there is a great difference between racial sentiment and racism.[22] Negritude is basically race consciousness, which was

Figure 7.17 Eugene Grigsby. *No Vacancy.* Woodcut. Reproduced by courtesy of Eugene Grigsby.

rudely awakened in the West Indian whose attitude was different from that of the Black American, Brazilian and Cuban due to the politics of extreme assimilation of Gallicanism and whitening, and for which a price had to be paid. Products of mixture of three races—black, white and red, brought up in Latin culture, ignorant of the history of their own country, of their continent, the history of the black race and the American Indian, they ended up by turning towards the element from which they could derive honor and pride.

20. Waters, *Masked Gods,* p. 37, 39.
21. Leon G. Damas, "Negritude in Retrospect," *Curricular Approaches to African and African-American Studies,* ed. E. W. Eko (Greensboro: Six Institutions' Consortium, 1970), p. 3.
22. Ibid., p. 5.

Figure 7.18 Alonzo Davis. Untitled. Oxidized steel and
rope. Reproduced by courtesy of Alonzo Davis and from
the collection of Rogers Recreational Center, Inglewood,
California.

. . . the systematic contempt in which white America held blacks, forced them to look to the past of the black race for motives of pride, historically, culturally and socially. In this way, the idea of race was a necessity in solving the ethnic problem of the U.S.A., and soon after the abolition of slavery, became a preoccupation for them.[23]

Damas outlines periods of development necessary to arrive at a viable self-image for a group.

First a period of indispensible acquisitions during which the blacks imported from Africa had to learn a new language and adapt to a new situation. A period of the absorption of black elements by the whites. A period of docile imitation of their models. . . . The second period was that of the anti-slavery struggle, which produced a literature of controversy, of moral and religious protest. The third period witnessed the accession of blacks to "real" culture, with two opposing tendencies. . . .[24]

It cannot be stressed too vigorously that there was a close relationship, though not always obvious, between Black artists employing various art forms. The search for self-identification was led by the writers, poets, and novelists and supported by musicians, dancers, painters, and other artists.

It was not until the 20's and 30's that there arose a generation of individual writers who no longer voiced cries of complaint and hope, but substituted demands for justice and openly determined to make them known. They affirmed clearly the quality of blackness, its entitlement to civil and cultural rights which DuBois defended so eloquently.[25]

Visual support for this growing affirmation of self-pride is seen in the paintings of Edwin Harleston, Archibald Motley, Laura Waring, William Farrow, James Porter, Lois Jones, and Hale Woodruff, and in the sculptures of Sargent Johnson, Augusta Savage, Mike Bannern, and Richmond Barthe, William Artis, and others. Langston Hughes spoke for all the artists in his Manifesto of 1926.

"We, creators of the new generation, we want to examine our black personality, without shame or

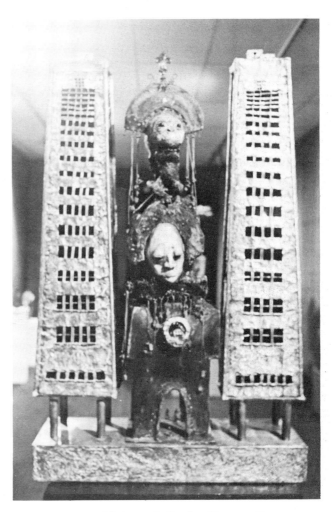

Figure 7.19 Geraldine McCullough. *Housing Project Totem.* Welded sheet copper, ceramic, glass, string, 57 x 28 x 60 inches. Reproduced by courtesy of Geraldine McCullough and from the collection of Cornell University.

fear. If it pleases the whites, we are very happy. If it does not please them, it does not matter. We know that we are beautiful, and ugly too. The tom-tom cries, the tom-tom laughs. If it pleases the men of color, we are very happy. If it does not it matters little. This is why we are building our temples, solid temples as we know how to erect, and we shared ready at the mountain top, moving freely."[26]

23. Ibid., p. 6.
24. Ibid.
25. Ibid., p. 7.
26. Ibid.

Figure 7.20 Hale Woodruff. *The Art of the Negro,* "Artists." Mural, panel six. The Negro artist has achieved eminence in various times and places throughout history. Here are muses symbolizing the cultural backgrounds which have characterized the works of artists. Artists represented include: Joshua Johnston, colonial portraitist; Henry O. Tanner, religious painter; Jacob Lawrence, contemporary painter; Edward M. Bannister, landscapist; Nada-Kane, South African cave painter; Julian Hudson, 19th century portraitist; Juan de Pareja, disciple of Murillo; "The Little One," 18th century sculptor; Igueigha, 13th century sculptor; Horace Pippin, 20th century primitive painter; Sargent Johnson, 20th century sculptor; Charles Alston, 20th century sculptor and painter; H. Hyppolite, 20th century Haitian primitive painter; Robert Duncanson, landscapist; and Richmond Barthe, 20th century sculptor. Reproduced by courtesy of Hale Woodruff and the Atlanta University and from the collection of the Atlanta University.

The fact that some communication existed between Black people of the United States, West Indies, Brazil, and Africa is little known, yet this contact was never completely broken. The arrival of new boatloads of slaves, often with stops in the West Indies, with some being held on the islands before being shipped to North or South America, served to keep thin lines of communication alive. The attitude of "Black pride" or "Negritude" was born in the exchange between Blacks of the West Indies, Africa, and the Americas. Aimeé Cesaire, born in Martinique, is said to have first expressed it; Leopold Senghor, poet and later president of Senegal, is said to have enlarged upon the idea with support; and contributions were made by Birago Diop and Leon Damas. Damas states that this group, which came together in Paris, was determined to follow the footsteps of Langston Hughes, Countee Cullen, Jean Toomer, Sterling Brown, Claude McKay, and Walter White. Hughes acknowledged and encouraged this relationship when he wrote:

> We are related—you and I
> You are from the West Indies
> I from Kentucky
> We are related—you and I
> You from Africa
> I from the States
> We are brothers—you and I[27]

The framers of "Negritude," led by Etienne Lero, flirted with surrealism for a while. Damas said they borrowed from the surrealist movement but never lost sight of their origins. He went on to say that

> . . . we were first of all by instinctive reaction, against Western civilization and the class of lyrism which Lero himself condemns soundly. In the wake of his efforts, we retained like him not only the range of works of Lautreamont, Rimbaud, Breton, etc., but firstly the works of the Afro-American writers."[28]

Damas claims that Lero gave a surrealist form to "Creole poetry" and made it possible for *Negritude* to rediscover the sense of our African personality.

At the end of World War II . . . a great cry went up, shaking the western world to its very roots.

The resounding voice of black men, for so long shunted aside, was at last making itself heard in a stupified world. . . . Negritude, in our interplanetory era, is a means and not an end.[29]

Writers, having words as their tools of expression, pinpoint ideas in such a poignant way that painters and sculptors so often leave for the viewer to interpret. Hughes pinpoints some of the dilemma felt by the Black person in America who sought to be a part of the mainstream. In *The Big Sea*, the first of several autobiographies, he tells the story of his own family with all its ethni-mixtures; White grandparents, Indian chiefs, Cherokee, Jewish, Scotch, French, and Negro. The fact that he is identified as Negro or Black is not based on the fact that most of his ancestors were Black or Negro, but that some of them were. Negro is defined as "any person with some Negro ancestors," and that "some" could be limited to *one!*

This explains in part, the complexion and hair texture of the American Negro or Black who range in color from jet black to white. It is not surprising that some Black people have identity problems, particularly those who don't look very Black. In early United States history, there were attempts to define the degree of Blackness or African heritage with terms like "mulatto," "octoroon," and "quadroon." In some places this manner of identification still exists, particularly in Brazil. Part of the objective for such classification was to separate and divide the allegiance of Black people and to create conflict among them by making the lighter ones feel superior to the blacker ones. For years these tactics were successful and, to a degree, still are. Many fair-complexioned Blacks felt superior to their darker relatives and separated themselves socially. Many of the lighter ones, sons and daughters of slave owners, were often provided better education and social position. Some were given a European education. To

27. Langston Hughes, "Brothers," *Montage of a Dream Deferred* (New York: Henry Holt, 1951). Copyright 1951 by Langston Hughes. Reprinted by permission of Harold Ober Associates Incorporated.
28. Damas, "Negritude in Retrospect," p. 10.
29. Ibid., p. 11.

Figure 7.22 Jeff Donaldson. *Ancestor Spirit #1*. Watercolor and aluminum foil. Reproduced by courtesy of Jeff Donaldson.

Figure 7.21 Doyle Foreman. Untitled. Bronze. Reproduced by the courtesy of Doyle Foreman.

be Black and African was a stigma that was a carry-over from slavery and many Black people resented being called Black. The easiest way to create a fight, before the advent of the 1960s civil rights movement, was to call a person Black. Hughes cites the case of a pantryman working on a ship with him while in an African port. The Africans could not accept Langston Hughes as Black and called him White, although Hughes insisted that he was Black. When the pantryman, who was quite dark, was referred to as Black, he rebelled, ". . . don't point at me." George said, "I'm from Lexington, Kentucky, U.S.A., and no African blood nowhere."[30]

Hughes cited another incident, when in a newspaper column he used the term Black to describe a New Jersey minister. The minister denounced Hughes to his congregation. Commenting on the incident, Hughes wrote

> They prefer to be referred to as brownskin or at the most as *dark brownskin,* no matter how dark they really are.[31]

Langston Hughes, who was of tan complexion, was one of the first poets to refer to himself as Black as equated with Negro when he wrote

> I am a Negro
> Black as the night is black,
> Black like the depths of my Africa.[32]

This declaration set the stage for an identification that helped polarize the thoughts of many Black intelligensia in the Americas and even to influence Africans. No matter the color of skin, it was that matter of a single African ancestor, often called African blood, that forced a community of identification between all who possessed it and created an American *Black experience.* From Harlem in New York to Watts in Los Angeles, from Beal Street in Memphis to wherever a sizable population of Black people were to be found, attitudes of White-created codes and conditions forced Black people into common communities.

Figure 7.24 Hale Woodruff. *Returning Home.* Linocut. Reproduced by courtesy of Hale Woodruff and the African Arts Magazine.

Ethnic ghettos are common in American cities, especially in large urban areas. Immigrants banded together in the older, economically impoverished areas with poor housing, lack of facilities, and poor schools. For the European immigrant, the tenure in these ghettos was relatively short as they moved up the economic ladder and improved their living conditions. For the Black, mobility was difficult, no matter what the economic condition. The Indian experienced much the same, or more, with isolation on the reservation. The Mexican-American or Chicano ghetto was less obvious but just as effective. As a result, those who lived or still live in such ghettos—real or imagined—have experienced an exchange of

30. Harold R. Isaacs, "Five Writers and their Ancestors" (Paper presented to the Third Annual Conference of the American Society of African Culture, University of Pennsylvania, June 22-26, 1960), p. 13.

31. Langston Hughes, *The Big Sea* (New York: American Century Series Hill and Wang, 1940), pp. 102-104.

32. Langston Hughes, *African Forum*, p. 17.

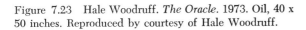

Figure 7.23 Hale Woodruff. *The Oracle.* 1973. Oil, 40 x 50 inches. Reproduced by courtesy of Hale Woodruff.

Figure 7.25 Hale Woodruff. *Three Tiered Gate*. 1974. Oil, 40 x 45 inches. Reproduced by courtesy of Hale Woodruff.

cultural patterns out of which has come artistic expressions of the ethnic community: Black, Indian, and Mexican-American.

The Harlem Renaissance

Langston Hughes writes that 1928 was a banner year for Harlem authors when the Negro vogue in the arts reached its peak.[33] The period is known as the Harlem Renaissance and its influence was felt by Blacks in Europe as well.

In France as well as Germany, before the close of the Negro Renaissance, Harlem's poets were already being translated. Leopold Sedar Senghor of Senegal and Aimeé Cesaire of Martinique, the great poets of *negritude*, while still students at the Sorbonne, had read the Harlem poets and felt a bond between themselves and us. In faraway South Africa, Peter Abrahams wrote in his autobiography, *Tell Freedom*, how, as a teenager at the

33. Langston Hughes, "The Twenties: Harlem and its Negritude," *African Forum*, I, no. 4 (1966):11-20.

Bantu Men's Social Center in Johannesberg, he discovered the Harlem poets of the twenties.[34]

The Harlem poets were unaware of the term *negritude* " . . . but certainly pride of heritage and consciousness of race was ingrained in us."[35]

Welded together by the fire of racism and economic deprivation and the insatiable desire to create, inspired by Black musicians and a Black musical tradition that stretched back to Africa, and inspired by a series of poets, preachers and protest writers extending back before the Civil War, isolated artists across the country were drawn, as if by magnet, to Harlem and burst forth in creative energy during the decades of the 20s and 30s shaping and forming a new ethnic aesthetic. Poets, painters, sculptors, novelists, essayists, playwrights, scenic designers, singers, dancers, musicians, and actors struggled to keep alive and took any kind of job. Some worked in menial jobs, and some worked as teachers, preachers, or musicians; but through all the difficulties, most kept in close touch with one another to exchange ideas and critical comment, which gave rise to and nutured the Black creative renaissance.

Harlem served as a magnet and spawning ground for young, Black creative talent. It also served as a source of talent for other communities. Alain Locke's writings spread the word of what was happening in Harlem, and universities and communities sought the aid of its artists. Howard University in Washington, D.C., Atlanta University, Dillard University in New Orleans, Fisk University in Nashville, and the Karamu House in Cleveland, Ohio were among those recognizing the importance of developing creative expression of the Black experience through visual and performing arts.

The Harlem Renaissance did not just happen. It was primed by academic thought and the Black intelligentsia. W.E.B. DuBois, one of the prime movers, had received a Ph. D. degree from Harvard in 1896 and did further work in Heidelberg, Germany. Academically he was a sociologist, but he also was a novelist and poet as well. As editor of the *Crisis*, official magazine of the National Association for the Advancement of Colored People with headquarters in Harlem, he gave outlet to many young Black writers and artists. DuBois also had a lifetime interest in Africa and African culture and attended the first Pan-African Congress in London in 1920, where West Indians, Africans, and American Negroes, exchanged points of view about the Black experience. DuBois was responsible for initiating and leading all subsequent Pan-African Congresses through 1945.[36]

Others who inspired or participated in the Harlem Renaissance included Paul Lawrence Dunbar whose works were well known to Countee Cullen, who had come from Kansas to write his poetry. Claude McKay had come from Jamaica to live, write, and influence young artists of all fields. Walter White, from Atlanta, contributed *Fire In The Flint*, a powerful novel of protest. Langston Hughes, from Kansas, called DuBois, Locke, and James Weldon Johnson the deans of the *New Negroes*, the first of whom he identifies as Claude McKay. Hughes arrived at the beginning of the renaissance at only nineteen years of age and wrote that, when he stepped off the Lennox Avenue subway, he looked around hoping to see Duke Ellington, Bessie Smith, or Bojangles Bill Robinson or Paul Robeson or Bert Williams walking down the avenue. He also hoped to meet famous writers and editors like McKay, Johnson, and DuBois, and also George S. Schuyler, Walter White, Jesse Fauset, or Eric Waldron from the West Indies. He was sorry to have missed Marcus Garvey, but Ethel Waters was still singing in Harlem nightclubs and Noble & Sissle's *Shuffle Along* was playing on Broadway.

Aaron Douglas from Kansas was painting his exotic silhouettes; Richmond Barthe from Louisiana was beginning to mold clay for bronze; Charles Gilpin had played "Emperor Jones" in Provincetown; and Paul Robeson was making his concert debut in Greenwich Village. Hall Johnson was gathering his famous choir; Countee Cullen was publishing his sonnets; and Zora Neal Hurston was writing her first stories. Mamie, Bessie, and Clara Smith were recording the "blues" and Duke Ellington and his "Jungle Band" were at the Kentucky Club, later the Cotton Club, where Negro patrons were not welcome unless they were very rich or very famous, like Bojangles Robinson.

34. Ibid., p. 17.
35. Ibid., p. 18.
36. Julius K. Nyerere, "Julius K. Nyerere's Speech to the Congress," *The Black Scholar* (July/August, 1974):19.

J. P. Johnson, Dan Burley, and Fats Waller were playing house-rent parties. Of all the personalities Hughes mentions, Paul Robeson is the only one who had been outstanding as an athlete. Robeson, a Phi Beta Kappa from Rutgers, had been a four-letter athlete and the first Black to be chosen on Walter Camp's All American Football team. Although he was a lawyer, Robeson became famous as a concert singer and later as an actor with a brilliant stage performance on Broadway as *Othello*. At the height of a brilliant career, he professionally and financially turned his back on success to speak out about injustices against less fortunate Black people.

The Black press, word of mouth, and other means of communication kept Black artists informed of developments in the various arts and how social conditions influenced the development of the arts. These modes of communication were the only ones open to review works by Black artists, for seldom was notice of their works included in the major presses, newspapers, magazines, or professional journals.

In most urban centers in the United States, Black people were strictly confined, by law and custom, to ghetto living. It was not until after the violent 1960s that there was an attempt to recognize works, whether mainstream or blackstream in content, by artists who happened to be Black. Ghetto living was not all negative as it reinforced certain cultural attributes of the Black experience. In many communities one went from first grade to university within the same community, making little contact with people of different ethnic backgrounds. Hardly any schools and few colleges of these communities offered courses in the arts until after the Great Depression, and then the few that did were staffed by artists inspired or developed during the Harlem Renaissance. There was even one foundation that supported and promoted the development of these artists.

The Harmon Foundation was a pioneer and catalyst for the support and development of many of these painters and sculptors. Hale Woodruff and Palmer Hayden were among the early ones to receive Harmon awards to study in Paris. Woodruff had been a student at the John Herron Art Institute before receiving the award to study in Paris. Both he and Hayden remained in Paris several years before returning to the United States. Hayden returned to live and work in New York, and Woodruff was persuaded by Dr. John Hope (a Black man who looked White), the president of Atlanta University, to leave Paris and to teach at Atlanta University. Woodruff protested that he was not a teacher and had no teaching credentials, but Dr. Hope saw a man of talent and leadership in him. In Atlanta, Woodruff inspired a long line of artists, many of whom became teachers of art.

Unlike Tanner, whom he admired, Woodruff immersed himself in the new developments that were taking place in Paris. The Cubists, Fauves, and other art movements were avidly studied and the best known of his early paintings, *The Card Players,* shows strong Cubist influence. When Woodruff returned to the United States, his works concentrated on the condition of the Black people of Atlanta. His paintings and woodcuts of the period depict the life of Black people, and these works are elevated above the usual genre painting due to his understanding of design and basic aesthetics. Mainstream critics have yet to appreciate the power of these early works. After nearly twenty years of teaching Black youth at Atlanta University, Woodruff moved to New York University after World War II where he became a major influence on a wider range of students both Black and White. The ethnic quality of his work has been muted to some degree but still remains as an underlying basis of his more abstract, fluid, and colorful painting. There was never the strong or blatant element of "protest" in his work. Instead, by the means of strong design, he conveyed the sometimes biting and sometimes humorous expression of the *Black experience*.

Protest as an art form was not a part of the lexicon of the Black visual artists. It was used mainly by the literary artists, especially the poets and, to a lesser degree, by the novelists and playwrights long before the civil rights movement that began in the 1950s.

8 Three Aspects of Ethnic Art: Folk, Academic, and International

The astronauts' view from their spaceships, high above the planet Earth, dramatically showed to them and to those receiving the televised picture the United States and the countries where a majority of those who populate this country came from. For the first time, the physical obstacles—oceans, deserts, and mountains—were clearly seen within the same picture frame. The United States is unique among modern nations, because few countries have condensed the original inhabitants into a small geographic area and repopulated the territory that they held with immigrants and their descendants in the short span of four centuries. It is as if the body of land had been emptied of its original inhabitants and had received an almost total transfusion of population, most of whom came from Europe and Africa. And these lands could all be seen from the astronauts' cockpit at the same time. This transfusion of population brought people from different cultures and with them came a variety of attitudes, beliefs, and arts. Beliefs, which they continued to express, and arts, which they continued to practice in varying degrees whenever possible, were both basically ethnic in nature. Art forms were perpetuated through practice and by instruction, which tended to maintain their ethnic identity. The European mode was dominant and strongly resisted outside influence.

During the first two and a half centuries, conditions of freedom and slavery served to reinforce ethnic conditions. The bulk of free people came largely from Europe and the slaves from Africa; mostly the free were White and the slaves were Black. From the first landings on the eastern shores, the new populations began pushing the original inhabitants, called "Indians," westward. Indians were color-coded "Red." These Indians, people with a well-defined civilization marked with unique art forms, were ethnically different from the newcomers. They were gradually pushed into limited geographic areas or contained in desolate areas where they were expected to perish. The "Red people" had their own ideas about life, death, religion, and beauty. Their tradition of the arts—dance, music, oral tradition, and visual arts—helped to shape their lives and to determine their actions in meeting the exigencies of life and death.

Each of these three major groups of people—Europeans, Africans, and Indians—are largely responsible for peopling the United States and, through centuries of cultural formation, developed strong attitudes of form and beauty and of good and bad. They had also developed feelings of friend and foe and a sense of self and group. They had a strong and well-developed cosmogony of their origin that shaped the ethnic quality of their arts.

Folk Art

The majority of the immigrants were fleeing oppression in Europe and seeking a land of opportunity. The majority of slaves were captives of war and were brought by force. Few of either group were professional artists and the arts first practiced by early immigrants were self-taught and nonprofessional. The results are generally classed as "folk art," or popular

Figure 8.2 Joshua Johnston. *Benjamin Yoe and Son.* Reproduced by courtesy of the Museum of Early Southern Decorative Arts, Winston-Salem, North Carolina.

art by and for "the folks." Most of these arts were comprised of useful objects necessary to carry on everyday affairs of the community and may not have been considered as "art" by the makers. In the same sense as the Indian and African, the immigrants did not look upon their art products as works divorced from everyday life to be viewed for intrinsic value alone. Certainly among many contemporary artists there is a resistance to include folk arts or crafts as "valid" arts. Individuals became skillful through practice and apprenticeship. They planned and built structures for living and working, and they made tools and utensils of clay and metal for farmers,

houseworkers, and shopkeepers. They made pictures which were drawn, painted, or stitched. They produced sculptures out of wood, metal, stone, and bone and made furnishings for the house.[1] Jean Lipman writes that,

The seeds of the native folk tradition, planted with the founding of the American colonies in the seventeenth century, sprouted and throve all along

1. Jean Lipman and Alice Winchester, *The Flowering of American Folk Art* (New York: Viking Press with Whitney Museum of Art, 1974), p. 9. Copyright 1974 in all Countries of the International Copyright Union by the Whitney Museum of American Art. Reprinted by permission of The Viking Press, Inc.

Figure 8.1 Alan Houser. *Navajo.* Steel, 1972. From the collection of the Heard Museum, Phoenix, Arizona.

the eastern seaboard from the last quarter of the eighteenth century through the first three quarters of the nineteenth. Folk art was a prime product of the new American democracy, strongly representative of the spirit of the country.[2]

She rejects such stylistic terms as primitive, pioneer, naive, natural, provincial, self-taught, and amateur as satisfactory labels of "folk art," but she suggests that the folk arts had

> . . . some common denominators: independence from cosmopolitan, academic traditions; lack of formal training, which made way for interest in design rather than optical realism; a simple and unpretentious rather than sophisticated approach, originating more typically in rural than urban places and from craft rather than fine-art traditions.[3]

In the preface, she comments on the striking relationship between some folk art and twentieth-century fine art and that some twentieth-century artists were collectors of folk art because of these similarities. Her comments close with the conviction

> . . . that the entire field of activity of the folk artist was absolutely not, as has often been said, a charming postscript. I believe it was a central contribution to the mainstream of American culture in the formative years of our democracy.[4]

Alice Winchester, in the same volume, defines American folk art

> In simplest terms, American Folk Art consists of paintings, sculpture and decorations of various kinds, characterized by an artistic innocence that distinguishes them from works of so-called fine art or the formal decorative arts.[5]

She admits that folk art is an imprecise, even subjective designation.

> Properly speaking, folk art is a traditional, often ethnic expression which is not affected by the stylistic trends of academic art. . . . Indeed, the line that separates it from academic art is not always

sharp and clear; there is a wide borderland in which they merge and overlap.[6]

Winchester quotes Maxim Karolik, a Russian who collected folk art, defending folk art to critics who label it merely "bad art."

> "One wonders whether, from the artistic point of view, the question I continue to ask is whether lack of technical proficiency limits the artists' ability to express his ideas. I do not believe it does. . . ."[7]

Lipman and Winchester have purposely made certain major omissions to what they term American folk art. These omissions include utilitarian objects, such as wooden scythes and wrought iron trivets, Spanish-American art of the Southwest, and the distinctive art of the American Indian.[8] Thus the art produced by the original inhabitants of the country and works by the Mexican-Americans, who have some stylistic affinity with the American Indian, are not a part of the volume. This parallels the attitudes that emptied the lands that the Indians held and furthers the sense of "colonization" as expressed above.

The inclusion or omission of works by artists of African heritage is not so clearly stated. No special mention is made concerning the omission of these works as is noted of the Indian and the Mexican-American of the Southwest. One work by a slave gives the impression that works of Black artists are included on the same plane as other "folk artists." Those familiar with the folk artists of African heritage will note the omission of works by such artists as Joshua Johnson, the Baltimore limner, whose works are found in the Salem, North Carolina museum and the National Gallery; Scipio Moorehead, engraver; and Thomas Day, cabinetmaker. Also missing is the fact that many creators of decorative ironworks

2. Ibid., p. 6.
3. Ibid.
4. Ibid., p. 7.
5. Ibid., p. 9.
6. Ibid.
7. Ibid.
8. Ibid., p. 8.

Figure 8.3 William H. Johnson. *Still Life*. Circa 1927.
Oil on canvas. Reproduced by courtesy of Smithsonian
Institution National Collection of Fine Arts.

Figure 8.4 William H. Johnson. *Sun Setting, Denmark.* Circa 1930-1935. Oil on burlap. Reproduced by courtesy of Smithsonian Institution, National Collection of Fine Arts.

in New Orleans, Charleston, and Mobile were slaves or Black freedmen.[9, 10]

The one piece that is included and identified as being by a Black person is a sculpture of a cigar-store Indian, whose creator is identified as Job, a slave active around 1825. This figure has features strongly reminiscent of masks from the central region of Zaire, Africa. Although this is the only figure identified in the catalog as being made by a slave, several other objects by anonymous artists might have been done by slaves or free Black artisans, judged by the shape and decoration of the works. Many craftsmen of early America, until the exclusion of Black artisans by craft unions, were known to have been Black. A great amount of research is needed to identify these craftsmen and their works.

This exhibit of folk art is typical of art exhibits in the United States in that they tend to omit works by artists of African, American Indian, and Spanish-American heritage and almost exclusively include only those of European ethnic backgrounds. Concerning this folk art exhibit, the effect is even more insidious inasmuch as no mention is made, other than the reference to Job, of the contribution to folk art by people of African heritage. One might ask if such designation is necessary or even desirable. The reply would have to be that the self-image of youth and

9. James Porter, *Modern Negro Art* (New York: Dryden Press, 1943), p. 23.
10. Elsa H. Fine, *The Afro-American Artist* (New York: Holt, Rinehart, and Winston, 1973), p. 22.

others in the community is based, to a large degree, upon models seen in the course of intellectual development. The inclusion of contributions made by all members of a society is a duty when such inclusive titles as "American Folk Art" are used. To do otherwise is to castrate a group and to deny them any knowledge of their ancestors.

In comparison, this appears to be a minor fault when considering the works of such a major historian as Sir Kenneth Clark. His book, based on a series of television programs titled *Civilization,* actually turned out to be "European civilization" and not "civilization" as one might expect. There would be no argument with such works if the title would indicate that the author is speaking of European civilization only. But the given implications are that only these are the works of civilized people and that all the rest are savage or uncivilized. Again, it is the colonial or colonizing mentality that permeates these writings.

The problem of including works by non-European peoples is not difficult or impossible. James Porter[11] pioneered the research done on the contribution of the Negro to handicrafts and the graphic and plastic arts from 1724 to 1900. He devotes the first chapter of *Modern Negro Art* to craftsmen of the pre-Civil War days by describing the contributions of African slave artisans to American folk art. Porter cites a remark from Peterson's *History of Rhode Island,* "That in some parts of the New England Colonies the Negro artist may be counted among the pioneers of American portraiture." And that Gilbert Stuart, ". . . derived his first impression of drawing from witnessing Neptune Thurston, a slave . . . sketch likenesses on the head of casks."[12] Porter cites that painters, etchers, engravers, architects, and cabinetmakers were in demand for the quality of their work. Thomas Day, a cabinetmaker from the vicinity of Charleston, South Carolina, was sought after by the ". . . richest clientele in Charleston and Virginia."[13] Day, a free Black man, was born in the West Indies during the late eighteenth century and was educated in Boston and Washington. His cabinetwork is identified by massive form and curvilinear line. A descendant of Thomas Day, W. A. Robinson, informed this writer that the famous "Day bed" gained its name from its maker, Thomas Day, rather than its function of being a bed by night and a couch by day.

James Porter emphasizes the ironworks created by Blacks ". . . in 1796 all the iron furnaces and forgers in Maryland were worked by Blacks."[14] A majority of pre-Civil War ornamental ironwork in Charleston and New Orleans was created by slave and free Black artisans.[15] Visitors to the South American city of Georgetown, Guyana cannot help but note the lacy filigree ironworks that adorn many of the older buildings of this city. These works were possibly created by Black artisans, which indicates a possible carry-over from skills learned in Africa.

Robert Farris Thompson has cited other folk art works found in Georgia and South Carolina that were produced by Black artisans. Thompson opined that although opportunities for slaves to continue producing plastic arts were more limited than traditions in music and dance, there is evidence that a folk art was practiced.[16]

The exhibition, The Flowering of American Folk Art, has purposely concentrated on arts that tend to have a strong European influence. The authors state that they have delimited arts of the American Indian and Mexican-American of the Southwest, but they make no mention of the African influence with the single exception of the Indian cigar-store figure by the slave, Job. Many unidentified creators of weathervanes, sculptures, fireplace decorations, boxes, clocks, and paintings are possibly creations by Blacks—slave or free—who were known to be skillful and active in these areas.

The identification of Black people, slave or free, is made because the general impression is held that all Black people were slaves. This is not exactly true, although a majority of them were held in bondage. A census of free "colored people" in the Charleston, South Carolina Directory of 1856 includes, among others, 50 tailors, 6 wheelwrights, 6 blacksmiths, 2 cabinetmakers, 4 dressmakers, 6 painters, 2 ship-

11. Porter, *Modern Negro Art,* pp. 13-28.
12. Ibid., p. 16.
13. Ibid., p. 9.
14. Ibid., p. 20.
15. Ibid., p. 22.
16. Robert Farris Thompson, "African Influence on the Art of the United States," *Black Studies In The University,* A. L. Robinson, C. G. Foster, and D. G. Oglive, eds. (New York: Bantam Books, 1969), pp. 128-177.

Figure 8.5 William H. Johnson. *Lamentation*. Circa 1939. Oil on board. Reproduced by courtesy of Smithsonian Institution, National Collection of Fine Arts.

wrights, 4 bootmakers, 1 molder, 1 tinsmith, 3 mattress makers, 1 jeweler, 1 silversmith, 1 carpenter, and 1 coffinmaker.[17]

. . . there was no dearth of vocations that could put to good use the artistic temperament and infinite capacity for taking pains that we call "craftsmanship." As boatload after boatload of Africans arrived in this country, memories of old-country techniques were constantly being refreshed by new arrivals from the Guinea coast. Thus, African skills and methods were preserved in this country even when other cultural elements were

being obliterated. And because art as craft so permeates African life and culture, aptitudes even survived several generations in this country.[18]

The development of folk art in the United States was grounded firmly in ethnic traditions and patterns which followed three founts of origin, Europe, Africa, and America. Forms of art, skills, and techniques

17. Judith Wragg Chase, *Afro-American Art and Craft* (New York: Van Nostrand Reinhold Co., 1971), p. 74.
18. Ibid., p. 75.

known in the Old World were changed to meet the needs of the new country. Just as the African blacksmith

> . . . might have been trained in making spears, iron money or anklets, he used the same techniques for making mule-bits, tin snips, or wrought iron gates. The basket-maker, the weaver, the potter, the leather-worker, probably had to make little adjustment between their former work and the new. The expert in bronze or brass could no longer make objects to glorify his king, but he had the basic skills for the transition to the job of brazier or silversmith.[19]

The transfer of skills, on the part of the European immigrant may not have been as drastic or as dramatic as that of his African counterpart, for he moved into a cultural milieu that was quite similar to the one from which he had come. There were, nevertheless, differences in form and function that necessitated changes in the handling of tools and materials to meet the needs of the New World.

Academic Art

If folk art can be characterized as artistically innocent, as traditional ethnic expressions, unlearned in a formal sense, and not affected by the stylistic trends of academic art, then academic art might be identified by the opposites, such as formalistic, sophisticated, perpetuated by institutions and institutional training, and having specific canons and rules to follow within a stylistic tradition. Originally the term indicated works of art emanating from the academy, particularly the French Academy. Although formalistic, stylistic, and sophisticated, academic art is no less ethnic than is folk art.

Just as the line between folk and academic art is not a sharp and definite one, the processes that achieve it are not sharp or definite. The general concept is that academic art is learned in a formal situation, in a school or by the apprentice method, whereas the folk artist is untutored either by school or apprenticeship, and they are all self-taught. In fact, many of the artists who fall under the academic classification have been self-taught, whereas a num-

ber of those classified as folk artists have served a period of apprenticeship and some have attended art schools. The earliest beginning of many academic artists was in the folk art tradition and some academically trained artists revert to what appears to be a folk art style or tradition. William A. Johnson, an artist of African heritage, is a good example. Born in Florence, South Carolina in 1901, he learned to draw by copying cartoons from local newspapers and ". . . knew from an early age that he must become an artist."[20] He managed to save enough money to pursue the five-year course at the National Academy of Design. Johnson won some of the top prizes while at the Academy, including the much coveted Canon prize in 1924 and again in 1926, the Hallgarten prize in 1925, and five other Academy prizes.[21] Breeskin tells us that Charles Hawthorne, a teacher of Johnson, felt strongly that he should have won the European travel fellowship, but the cards were stacked against him because he was Black. Hawthorne sought to raise a fund equivalent to the amount of the traveling fund. While he waited for this financial aid, Johnson took lessons from George Luks. When Hawthorne's efforts were successful, Johnson went to Paris, where he remained at least three years.[22]

During his stay in Paris, Johnson came under the influence of Chaim Soutine, the expressionist painter, and was strongly influenced by him. Subsequent years of poverty and struggle in Europe, marriage to a Danish woman, and travel to North Africa changed the nature of his painting from that of an academic to a folk style.

> Johnson found the contrast between Europe and Africa just as great as between America and Europe. Because he looked like an Arab, he was welcomed in the natives' homes and learned to love their peaceful way of living and their extreme simplicity. He was convinced that such simple

19. Ibid.
20. Adelyn Breeskin, *William H. Johnson 1901-1970* (Washington: Smithsonian Institution Press, 1971), p. 11.
21. Ibid.
22. Ibid., p. 12.

people understood the meaning of art better than the so-called cultivated people because, "we are . . . closer to the sun. . . ."[23]

Academic art is generally considered under the narrow limitations of the representational, realistic tradition that is taught in the academies. The academy uses the Greco-Roman tradition as a model, a tradition which came to full bloom in Europe during the Renaissance and was crystalized in the academic schools of Europe during the early nineteenth century. I would propose a broader interpretation of academic art. My interpretation would include art that is distilled into specific formalized traditions and passed on to students or apprentices in order to perpetuate the tradition. In this sense the various schools of "modern art" would come under the umbrella of academic art, as well as the many self-perpetuating art movements. All of these schools or developments are basically ethnic in nature, with the exception of what is termed extreme "intercontinental art."

Based upon the hypothesis that academic art is fundamentally ethnic, the earliest recognized traditions in the history of Western art, that of Egypt, has all the elements of ethnicity. Architecture, painting, sculpture, crafts, jewelry, pottery, and costume attest to the rigid canons of design and meaning in the art produced. Furthermore, it was basically a religious art.

Greek, Roman, Etruscan, Assyrian, and arts of later Italian city-states are identifiable by geographic, religious, and "racial" components peculiar to works produced. College students quickly learn to distinguish between works produced in European countries of France, Germany, Holland, Denmark, Russia, England, and Spain. There is a similarity of content and form between the arts of these countries because there was considerable exchange between the artists. El Greco traveled from Greece to Italy where he studied and worked before going on to Spain. Durer visited and studied in Italy. These are two of the many examples of the exchange. The purpose here, however, is not to go into detailed descriptions of the art or artists of these countries, as these are well developed in most art history texts. It is sufficient to note that the quality of the art produced in a country tends to develop within a framework peculiar to that country. The development appears to move from folk art to academic art and

then to international art, with the first two, folk and academic art, retaining strong geographic components. Note, for example the similarities of the Dutch tradition in the works of Vermeer and Mondrian. The severity of line, pattern, rhythm, and movement maintain an affinity even though the content and surface structure are different. In each area, through apprenticeship or special schools, art students were taught techniques of handling materials according to tradition and more importantly were given attitudes and concepts that were passed on along with such techniques. These attitudes and concepts, ingrained for centuries, formed a background for the immigrants coming to the New World that influenced the content and form of the work produced by their decendants. One might say that the immigrants were "programmed" to produce the kind of art products that they created in the New World.

If the European immigrants were programmed in terms of art attitudes through informal folk arts and formal academic training in their native lands, the more reluctant immigrants, who were brought in chains from their native Africa, were equally programmed. Egypt, the original source and beacon of Western art, had gained much of its artistic style and content from the African interior where American slaves originated. Scholars have attempted for years to identify the inhabitants of Egypt as White or other than Black, but these arguments have been refuted by a number of scholars, particularly Cheikh Anta Diop. Diop has documented in great detail the sources of Egyptian civilization and, through a variety of measurements, documents, and deductions, has identified the Egyptian civilization and the rulers at the height of artistic developments as Black by tracing the influences of Egyptian art to the interior of Africa. Folk art and academic art, through apprenticeship and specific training, are found throughout the African continent.[24]

Justification of the slave trade and exploitation of foreign lands led European scholars to apply the terms "savage" and "primitive" to Africans, Indians,

23. Ibid., p. 14.
24. Cheikh Anta Diop, *The African Origin of Civilization: Myth or Reality,* ed. and trans. Mercer Cook (New York: Lawrence Hill and Company, 1974).

and other non-Europeans. Anthropologists, artists, and historians in recent years have attempted through research to reveal the nature of African and American Indian civilizations and the arts they produced. Their findings are in contrast to the picture given by colonists, land exploiters, and justifiers of the slave trade. The result of these findings is that the non-European, like the European counterpart, had developed a strong folk art tradition and a rigid, formal academic art based on tradition which was passed on from generation to generation through instruction, as well as an international art, which was accepted and understood within the tradition of the respective European, African, and American continents.

International Art

The term *international art,* as it is used here, must be considered in two dimensions. The first dimension is between nations of a continent and includes works having certain similar shapes and content which was recognized, accepted, and understood by nations or tribes within a continent. Thus, we can speak of the international aspect of African art, indicating that the arts of African nations are more similar to one another than they are to the arts of European, Oriental, or native American Indian nations within these respective continents. The concept of form, basic design, and ideational content of art from the African continent have points in common that differ greatly with the concept of form, basic design, and ideational content of art from other continents. Within the continent, however, there exist sharp differences between the works produced by people of one nation or tribe with those of another. Consequently, the works of the Yoruba are quite different from those of the Senufo; the French from the German; and the Kwakiutl from the Hopi.

The second dimension of *international* art, as it is used here, might be better termed *world* art or *intercontinental* art, a recent development, and is perhaps the result of improved communications and exchange of ideas globally. This art contains little or no ethnic components. A work created in New York, Tokyo, Lagos, or London reveals little or nothing of its geographical, racial, or religious origin.

Communications through electronic media, press, travel, and satellites have psychologically reduced the size of the world to the degree that perpetuation of folk and academic art have become threatened.

The increased interest in and production of *intercontinental* art has reduced the ethnic component to a minimum. The intercontinental artist has focused attention more on technical rather than human concerns and on perceptual rather than conceptual expression. The "expressive" factors, which relate to ideas and concepts carried by a work of art, are missing in most intercontinental art. Some highly symbolic works appear to fit the intercontinental mold but carry a strong ethnic message such as the works of Rubem Valentim which use symbols that represent the Yoruba Orisha Shango. Other works of this style, which are devoid of symbolism, cultural expression, or human dimensions, suggest a degree of anti-humanism. For art to be humanistic, it must relate in some way to a human perspective.

On one hand, the intercontinental style seems to have a potential for cementing relations between peoples. Works of this style are devoid of the provincial qualities of nationalism, racism, or religious dogma. Many do not completely negate cultural heritage, but they do attempt to assimilate the best aesthetic values from a variety of cultures. On the other hand, another side of intercontinental art seems to reject all traits of a society or cultural heritage and leaves nothing except a stark, cold, aesthetic product. Perhaps this is the ultimate of "art for art's sake." It may be considered an ideal to seek a sameness in works of art where products of all men are alike, with the implication that all men are brothers and all people are alike; just as the intercontinental art product from any point on the globe is alike. This may be an ideal concept but one that considers no individual differences, no ethnicity, no cultural heritage, and no feeling other than for aesthetic form and design. In spite of such a noble implication, there persists a gnawing sensation of a loss of individuality, which is the end result, like industrial products on an assembly line stamped out by the thousands and controlled from beginning to end by computer technology.

The artist has usually been a predictor of social change, and the increased interest in art without ethnic content, cultural input, or individual self-identity may be a prediction of the future shape of world society.

9 Conclusion

The United States has not turned out to be the "melting pot" of peoples as it once was predicted to become. Sharp differences remain between peoples of different origins after two hundred years of nationhood. Wars and laws, religion, schools, and intermarriage at one time or another have attempted to bring together people with strong differences of cultural and ethnic backgrounds. At times such means have been successful but more often, greater differences between peoples have been created. While one group worked for greater harmony, another created disharmony. Technology may be more successful where efforts by institutions have either failed or made very limited progress in melting the ethnic nuggets of peoples. This success, however, may come as a mixed blessing, bringing greater dissatisfaction than pleasure. The technological message is computer dictated, lacking in human compassion and likely to require a sameness or conformity of cultural expression. This could possibly create a unified culture out of all the different ones that now exist. On the other hand, for art and ethnics this message will mean the loss of image, loss of uniqueness, and loss of individuality. There should be some way to achieve national expressiveness without the loss of unique personalities.

The ethnic uniqueness that colors, flavors, and makes fragrant the streams of human personalities in this great country are slowly being blended into a homogenous oneness through modern technology, such as rapid tranportation, print and electronic media, programmed instruction, standardized achievement tests, standardized food packaging and convenience food stands, and standard identification of people by number rather than by name. These are but a few factors of computer culture melt and are the most noticeable movements toward a homogenous population, devoid of "soul" or perceptual sensitivity. The cyclic tempo of life moves at an ever-increasing rate and the spin-off of rejects—reflected by empty, dejected, and wasted human lives from all economic walks of life and all ethnic and cultural groups— with no sense of self-worth, knowledge of heritage, or respect for that of other people, is alarming. Youthful dropouts from school and adult dropouts from society often live aimless lives, unable to catch up with the future, to keep up with the present, or to understand the meaning of the past. They become dregs of society at worst, and at best, zombies responding only to the will of "Madison Avenue-like masters." Little better than slaves following each passing fad, these passive viewers of the "tube of life" do the bidding of the media masters who shape their programmed minds.

Computer technology may have improved the quantity of things we need but the quality has been impaired. Evidence of this surrounds us. Meats and vegetables have become tasteless ware wrapped in plastic on supermarket counters. Tasteless TV dinners look appealing in colorful commercials but are lacking in flavor. When cooking aromas dare invade the kitchen, handy aerosol sprays mask the interlopers with a singularly sickening smell. Electronic music shrills and assaults the hearing, or soft background music lulls with an anonymous drone devoid of personality. Loud or soft, the difference between selection is mainly in the title.

Even the structures where we live and work con-

Figure 9.1   Buildings in Brasilia, Brazil.

tinue to become more and more alike. Housing projects and row houses in economically deprived communities have always tended to look alike because it was cheaper to build them this way. Now "town houses" in affluent communities and suburban subdivisions take on "look-alike" features. Civic buildings across the nation, boxlike, beehive, and high-rise with reflective metallic glass windows, become repeats of one another. In many instances these new structures reflect a growing intercontinental style of architecture seen in many countries around the world. In most cities this style is seen in contrast with older structures of different periods that serve to enrich the cultural heritage. In "all new" cities there is an absence of the unique antique which serves as a cultural anchor.

Perhaps the most striking example of the intercontinental style is seen in the architecture of Brasilia, capital of Brazil, where impressive multistory buildings repeat themselves mile after mile. This is a strange, awesome city, that gives the feeling of being in outer space, linked with the future but not with the past. This feeling may have been one of the objectives of its designer-architect, Oscar Neimeyer. There is no sense of heritage or ethnicity in this new city, and there are no contrasting structures of

older design with which to relate. Adding to the awesomeness is the heroic scale of buildings and sculptures. One senses a city peopled by concrete giants who dwarf the human being. The scale is so grand that human beings are seldom seen or rarely noticed even in photographs. This monumental, impressive, intercontinental architecture of Brasilia seems to deny ethnicity and the human experience.

Other movements in art have tended toward this direction, but few have gone so far. Picasso and Braque were moving in this direction with analytical Cubism but reversed the trend with synthetic Cubism. Some artists continued to explore in the direction analytical Cubism was headed and produced paintings and sculptures which probed mainly the formal dimensions of aesthetics. The Russians, Kandinsky and Malevitch, and the Dutchman, Mondrian, were pioneers of this non-representational art, but their work seemed to maintain a flavor of cultural heritage. This sense of heritage is absent in such recent movements as op, minimal, and conceptual art. A reviewer of the exhibit, Eight Contemporary Artists, from Italy, Germany, Holland, Australia, and the United States at the Museum of Modern Art in New York complained that the exhibit makes one, "Vividly and depressingly aware of how intellectual art has become

Figure 9.2 A cathedral in Brasilia, Brazil.

and how estranged from basic human experience and perception."[1]

There seems to have always been a small, dedicated army of avant-garde artists who work to maintain aesthetic integrity and to probe what the shape and content of art might become. They have been in the forefront of major movements helping to effect change. Could it be that the avant-garde artists of today foretell the success of the "melting pot" and the equality of all United States citizens through artistic expression or through art forms which deny ethnic or cultural experiences? Could this not lead to the reduction of perceptual experience to an ultimate zero level? Could this also lead to computerizing and mechanizing of all art forms? The voices of the avant-garde may suggest such possibilities, but human nature does not support such predictions. Sharp divisions between human beings, which have ethnic, cultural, and economic roots,

unfortunately seem to indicate that greater differences are likely before complete "melting" occurs to produce a single unified expression of art or society.

Social and economic conditions are sharply etched between peoples of different cultures and ethnic backgrounds in the United States in spite of attempts to integrate schools, housing, employment, and places of amusement. Few racial and ethnic minorities, usually at the bottom of the economic ladder, live in integrated communities, whether by choice or for economic or social reasons. Even the more affluent majority, who move to suburbia, usually regroup along ethnic lines.

It would be a mistake to assume that the flow of migrants from the old ethnic neighborhoods to the

1. Diana Loercher, "Gloomy Outlook for Contemporary Art? New York Show Hints Yes," *Christian Science Monitor* (November 14, 1974):10.

124

suburb is always random. On the contrary, in many areas there are numerous suburban communities which are inhabited predominantly by persons of the same ethnic group. Hence, one finds Jewish, Polish and Italian suburbs in New Jersey, around Detroit, and in proximity to Providence and Boston.[2]

The persistency of ethnic neighborhoods exists throughout the United States but is seldom noticed until violence erupts as in bussing for forced integration or when incursions are made into religious enclaves sparked by textbook controversy. Kriskus traveled for a year and a half throughout the urban northeast and after much study concluded ". . . that the ethnic dimension is still a persistent behavioral factor in the lives of . . . Americans."[3]

Many native American Indians often find it difficult to adjust to living in urban centers and prefer life on the reservation even though life there may be physically more difficult. Most major cities have Black, Chicano, and Oriental communities and these are often divided into economic subdivisions. These communities, estranged and separated from the various White ethnic ones, present difficulties to teachers in their efforts to educate. Difficulties are sometimes compounded when youth of different ethnic backgrounds attend the same school.

Changing social conditions, pushed first by riots and then by laws, have reduced legal barriers in housing, education, jobs, and recreation. Different ethnic faces and voices are increasingly seen and heard in the classroom, in the marketplace, on the playing field, and on television. Hard-won court fights have created demands for art teachers and artists from minority ethnic backgrounds, and these demands outstrip the supply of people prepared to fill requests. Previous conditions have poorly prepared those outside the social and economic mainstream to meet the level of competency expected, since few opportunities for social or economic mobility have been available. Positions of importance in education, business, and industry have historically been held by European immigrants and their descendants who have jealously guarded and tenaciously held these positions. From the beginning there has existed a hierarchy in the arts in much the same sense as the hierarchy in society. This hierarchy has been basically ethnic, placing the European concept of art above that of other continents. The "pecking order"

Figure 9.3 Rip Woods. *Hunger.* Charcoal. Reproduced by courtesy of Rip Woods and the author and from the collection of the author.

2. Richard J. Kriskus, "The White Ethnics: Who Are They and Where Are They Going?" *City* 5, no. 3 (May/June, 1971): 25. Reprinted by permission from *City*, Magazine of Urban Life and Environment, May/June 1971. Copyright 1971. The National Urban Coalition, 1201 Connecticut Avenue, N. W., Washington, D.C. 20036. All rights reserved.

3. Ibid., p. 23.

followed social and economic dominance, and those at the top shaped the culture and society, dictated the values, and established the hierarchy even while bickering among themselves. From the very beginning the Puritans and the Pilgrims argued, while they held a tight rein on society.

Within the hierarchy of the arts, fine art and folk art were separate. The interrelation between the arts and society found among native American Indians or among African societies was not permitted. Art was either secular or sacred and these were kept separate. "Fine" music, or music of greatest value, was either symphonic or chamber music. Spirituals, jazz, and other music of African derivation was "vulgar." Most Oriental and all native American Indian music was ignored by the American taste makers. Dance was viewed in a similar fashion. The highest level was ballet, with folk and ballroom dancing being tolerated. Dances created by slaves and their descendants were to be avoided for they were vulgar. The shuffling of Indians could hardly be considered dancing at all. These attitudes, brought with the first settlers and maintained through popular writing, educational texts, and classroom teaching, persist today and become additional barriers for teachers to overcome when faced with students from different ethnic backgrounds and with attitudes different from their own. These barriers, great as they have been and still are, are not impossible to overcome.

It is important to note that many individual artists of non-European background, who fitted the expected mold and mastered the techniques of artistic hierarchy, were supported and given recognition for their attainment throughout the history of the country. Some have gained prominence and even fame, but few are to be found in textbooks or art histories. The list is much too long to repeat here, but a few random examples would include Phyllis Wheatley, a poet; Blind Tom, concert pianist; Maria Tallchief, ballet dancer; Marian Anderson, concert singer; Henry O. Tanner, painter; Edmonia Lewis, sculptor; Charles Gilpin, actor; and Paul Robeson, actor and singer. Lewis, Tanner and Gilpin, along with a number of other artists, found it necessary to leave the United States to gain success in their chosen fields.

Today the number of artists of non-European background in the United States is greater than ever before, but that number is still relatively small when compared with population figures showing percent-

ages of peoples with European and non-European backgrounds. One might ask why the percentage is small, and many reasons might be advanced in answer. Most of the reasons will be economic, but there are others as well. Three reasons, besides economic ones, persist—lack of opportunity, lack of models to emulate, and a desire to maintain ethnic identity rather than to be dominated by European-based norms or values.

The process of successful upward mobility in the United States through economic, class, cultural, social, and racial barriers is more difficult for those of non-European heritage than for persons of European background, and more for non-English-speaking people than for English-speaking people. The potential for success, when compared with that of other countries is greater here than in most countries. In spite of the hierarchy or economics, class and cultural barriers, and in spite of all the differences that exist between peoples of the country, the United States has provided greater opportunities for peoples of different cultural and ethnic backgrounds than any other country. One of the main reasons has been the educational system of the country. These may seem to be empty words to those on the bottom of the ladder, who have never seen or experienced the rigid class and economic structures, found in many other countries. We have no claim of perfection here, for the United States and its minority groups have yet to come near reaching their potential. Art teachers have an important role to play in the efforts to reach this potential which will surely strengthen the moral and spiritual fibers of the country through the development of greater understanding of the artistic heritage of peoples of different cultures for a greater sense of personal worth.

This potential is possible because the United States is a relatively young country, newly populated when compared with the countries of Europe, Asia, and Africa. Brazil, Argentina, and Australia may be similar in that they have also been infused with a majority of peoples of European background but the immigration has been more unitary: Portugese in Brazil, Spanish in Argentina, and English in Australia. Some European countries appear to offer greater freedom to individuals from the "Third World" than the United States does, but this appearance is misleading. Success is available to only a small percentage because the numbers of these peoples are severely limited and, as a group, they seldom become a political or social threat. As a result, only a few can be afforded special privilege.

In the "Origins of Population," cited earlier, no one group exceeded the 14.4% of the English. Roughly half of the United States population is European in origin with the remaining half divided between American Indians, Blacks, Orientals, and "others." Because of this diversity of origin, there is potential for conflict, and there is even greater potential for creative peaceful encounter. The schools are the most logical and best suited of all institutions to prevent conflict and develop creativity. The arts and the cultural backgrounds of this diverse population could serve well as a basis for this development. Of all the subjects, the arts are best suited for exploring and developing the uniqueness of individuals through the phenomenological approach of self-actualization.

The area of phenomenology that is relative to this discussion is the part that deals with the need of the individual for self-worth, self-respect, and a knowledge of and respect for his heritage. When this is denied, as it is in many blatant and subtle ways in our society, the result is self-demeaning, self-destructive, and a desire to destroy others. The individual denied self-worth, for whatever reason, is made to feel inferior while others around him are made to feel superior; both are destructive to the personality. When a genuine sense of self and self-worth is developed, one is more likely to develop respect for others. Such self-actualization would do much to promote integrity of self and confidence in others and could serve to improve the quality of education and of living for all peoples. This would not in any way solve the pressing social and economic needs of the country, but it would be a giant step forward. For those interested in pursuing this point, see Abraham Mazlow, *Toward a Psychology of Being* and Carl Rogers, *On Becoming a Person*.

In order to achieve this creative potential, for all groups of society, some changes will have to be made in the hierarchy of social structure. Although social and economic factors are tightly interwoven, social changes, difficult as they may be to overcome, are likely to be achieved more easily than economic ones. One major change that must be accomplished is that of greater recognition of non-European cultures and the arts they have produced. In achieving this step,

recognition must be made of non-European arts on the same level of importance as that which is European. Civilization, in other words, must be recognized in cultures beyond the limits of Sir Kenneth Clark. Works of art from Third World countries must not be required to fit the mold of the European value system, but they must be accepted for their own value. Value judgments must be broadened and criteria established for works of art that differ from the European norm. When peoples of different cultural and ethnic backgrounds and the works they have produced have been accepted as equally as that of the European, then there is the possibility of sharing and exchange of cultural components to create a new and vital art for a new "renaissance."

Such changes will be difficult, for they will require new ways of thinking about art and about people. They will require a relinquishing of "colonized minds" in the same way that "colonized lands" have been relinquished. The giving up of mental attitudes will be far more difficult than giving up lands. The lands that the colonials released in different parts of the world were no longer productive, or they were costing more than they were worth and were liabilities rather than assets. The minds that must be relinquished are assets with great creative potential.

These changes will be difficult for the art educators, for they will require shifts in priorities in teaching art history, studio, and art education classes. Fewer pages of texts would be devoted to arts of Europe and more to Third World countries. Individual artists of different cultural backgrounds, whose integrity has not permitted them to imitate the current European or Euro-American movement, will have to be identified and recognized. These changes will be great and even traumatic for some, including artists, educators, and those with vested interests in the status quo, but they won't be impossible. Indeed, these changes are taking place now and are being promoted in a variety of places with limited publicity. The benefits that these changes offer, are a self-actualized nation of differing peoples, stronger and healthier than ever, more like a "stew pot," a "Mulligan stew" if you will, and not a melting pot where all the different flavors are lost.

Once the individual or group develops a strong self-image, it will then be possible for one group to relate to, or negotiate with, other groups from a point of self-worth rather than from a superior/inferior position. Several institutions have been established with this concept. One of the most notable is the Institute of American Indian Arts in Santa Fe, New Mexico. Director Lloyd New, a Cherokee, developed the curriculum concept of teaching young Indians their cultural heritage as well as that of Europe and America. Through this institute would come a new concept of teaching that fused the two together. They fused Indian and Euro-American with foreign and traditional to form a new art. There have been some notable successes in meeting this objective and the students have explored new forms of art without losing a sense of heritage or without a threat of a loss of identity.

The Elma Lewis School of Art in Dorchester, Massachusetts and the Karamu House in Cleveland, Ohio are private schools which have promoted self-identification of Black youth through the study of the arts. This study merges contributions of different cultures in much the same way as the IAIA in Santa Fe.

These schools are exceptions to the general condition. Most artists have attended schools that gave little, if any, recognition to non-European-style arts. Artists from these backgrounds have had to master aesthetic concepts and technical skills of the majority culture before giving vent to expressions of their own heritage. Although many of the younger artists have eschewed this process, the mastery of such skills have strengthened aesthetically and technically those who have followed it. One of the best-known Black artists, Romare Bearden, has gone through a number of developments that graphically show the results of this technical mastery. He studied in traditional art schools in the United States and Europe and with individual artists. His style began with a stylized realism, moved to non-objectivism, and then to a highly personal realism which he now expresses through the medium of collage. His subject matter is the Black experience as he has perceived and experienced it. Like Walter White, Bearden is of light complexion, but with a burning compassion to make a personal statement which he does exceedingly well. His works are found in major collections and he was one of the first of the Black artists to be given a major one-man exhibition by the Museum of Modern Art in New York. He has raised the technique of collage to a major art form.

Hughie Lee-Smith studied at the Academy of

Design in New York and is now recognized for his interpretation of a personalized surrealist style of painting, vibrant with mystery and subtle connotations of human conditions. When asked his thoughts about "Black art" he stated that an artist must be sensitive and aware of what's going on in the world both socially and politically. "If one is immersed in the life around him, as in my case—in the life of black people and their struggle, then something is bound to come out that reflects this sensitivity." His thesis was that "the better one is able to use the tools and materials of the artist, the better one is able to shape and present an aesthetic concept whether this concept has ethnic dimensions or not."[4]

Rip Woods, an Arizona artist, has mastered this ability to handle media for a powerful expression. On the basis of this ability he was selected as the Arizona artist in the Denver Museum's 74th Annual Western Exhibit which included ten other artists from many states. Rudy Turk, Director of University Art Collections at Arizona State University, writes in the catalog that

> Painting, sculpture, prints and drawings are nuisance categories when viewing or criticizing the work of Rip Woods. They imply methods and techniques for creativity and re-creative responses that are inadequate for the fusion of artistic media which Woods uses to create his imagery. To present Woods as a painter or sculptor is equally ineffectual. Quite simply, Rip Woods is an artist, . . . and the criteria for judging his works is singly implicit in each of his works and not to be found among the conventionally accepted standards for aesthetic evaluation.[5]

What Turk does not include is that Woods has a strong self-image which forms a broad base for his creative imagery and exploration of a variety of media. He was raised by poor but strong, resourceful, and creative parents. As a high school art student, he was familiar with the works of such artists as Henry O. Tanner, Hale Woodruff, Jacob Lawrence,

4. Taped interview with Hughie Lee-Smith, 1970, unpublished.
5. Rudy Turk, "Rip Woods," The 74th Western Annual (Denver: The Denver Art Museum, 1973), pp. 7-12.

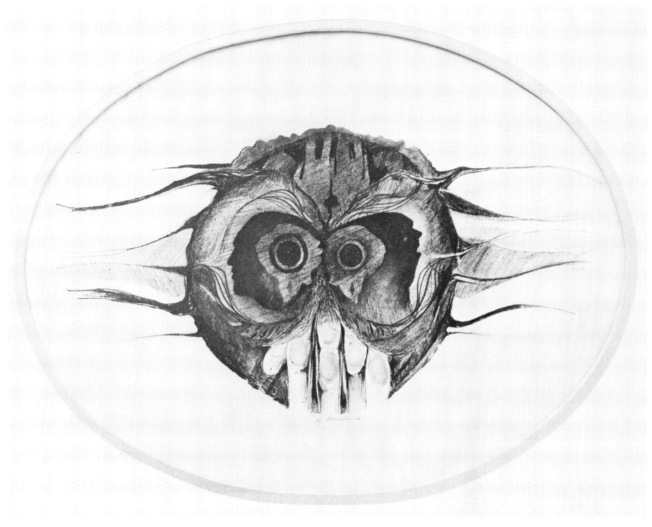

Figure 9.4 Rip Woods. *Un Beso de Amour.* Conte crayon and charcoal, 24 x 30 inches. Reproduced by courtesy of Rip Woods.

Charles Alston, and Romare Bearden, as well as being familiar with the usual European and American artists presented in art classes. When Woods managed to attend college, a great deal of his self-actualization had already been accomplished and, in part, because of this he was able to develop a unique manner of expression which is constantly changing. Like Hughie Lee-Smith, Woods believes one should master the tools and materials that one works with and let expression be based on one's sensitivity to the life experience. Woods calls himself "an artist who happens to be Black and who expresses the experience of a Black man to the best of my ability."

The New Mexico artist represented in the 74th Western Annual was Fritz Scholder. Robert A. Ewing notes in the catalog that

Fritz Scholder is, in the best sense of the word, an exploitive artist. He has a rare gift for analyzing the world in which he lives and gearing his work and his life style to match the times . . .
. . . Raised in a house where things Indian were played down as a negative aspect of life, he conceived a passion for the arts and acquired a vaulting ambition accompanied by his own furies. (One can imagine those Scholder furies—trailing tatters of beads and feathers— screeching after him across the skies enveloped in the unearthly din of bone whistles).

Two influences on his early painting symbolize the most important aspects of his mature work. A family move to South Dakota brought him into contact with Oscar Howe, the distinguished Sioux

Figure 9.5 Rip Woods. *Grass Moon*. Serigraph, 20 x 31 inches. Reproduced by courtesy of Rip Woods and from the collection of the Tucson Museum of Art.

painter, who reached beyond the limits of traditional Indian art to incorporate contemporary elements in his work. Later . . . he studied with Wayne Thiebaud, who rounded out his interest in the art of our time. . . . Enthusiastic participation in the Southwest Indian Art Project sponsored by the Rockefeller Foundation led to a teaching position at the Institute of American Indian Arts in Sante Fe. Scholder arrived in New Mexico in the mid 1960's determined to eschew the Indian as a subject. . . . While teaching at the I.A.I.A., he first painted a stripe series, followed by a brief dazzle of butterflies, before submitting to the inevitable subject matter which was to bring him the recognition which he craved.

. . . The fact is that from the fertile stew of the pre-Red Power I.A.I.A. he has been the only person to produce a major body of work which carries the Institute's initial thesis—the combination of Indian traditions and contemporary idiom—to a coherent conclusion. His Indian-ness (variously reported as one fourth, one eighth, and negligible) can only be doubted if one has never seen him or talked with him.

. . . The virile red genes dominate, and he *looks* and *thinks* Indian. His tenderness and arrogance, his antic sense of humor, his sharp will for life, his gift for the unexpected are all as Indian as parched corn and pemmican.[6]

An interview with R. C. Gorman, Navajo painter, expressed the cultural affirmation in a somewhat different way. Gorman, who masks his serious self with jokes and laughter, talks of the Navajos as the greatest of "rip-off" artists. ("Rip-off" is a term that came out of the Black community during the riots of the 1960s and means to boldly take or steal.)

6. Robert A. Ewing, "Fritz Scholder," The 74th Western Annual (Denver: The Denver Art Museum, 1973), pp. 47-54.

Figure 9.6   Fritz Scholder. *Study for Fierce Indian #2.*
Acrylic, 18 x 12 inches. Reproduced by courtesy of Fritz
Scholder and from the collection of the Elaine Horowitch
Gallery.

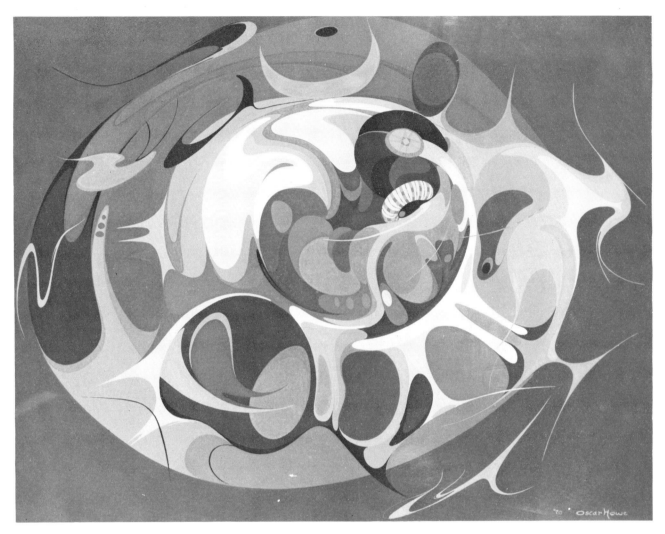

Figure 9.7 Oscar Howe. Untitled. From the collection of the Heard Museum, Phoenix, Arizona.

"We are famous for being thieves, everything the Navajo is known for has been stolen from other cultures: Navajo rugs, Navajo sand painting, Navajo jewelry; all of these were ripped-off from other tribes and from the Spanish. What we did was to develop it and make it better; we made them our own. Me, I'm the greatest rip-off of them all. Who did I rip-off? I don't know, maybe Walt Disney."[7]

The laughter which followed and the twinkle in his eye made the interviewer know that Gorman was half serious and that half had far deeper meaning than was immediately apparent. His paintings concentrate on a single theme, Navajo woman, reflecting his sensitivity to his heritage.

These are but a few of many artists who have found ways to present a personal as well as a universal self. They have reached a sense of freedom based on their

own self-worth and self-actualization. For each one mentioned above, ten other examples could be cited. Teachers and students should search out the lives of artists from a variety of cultural backgrounds to discover how they have achieved success. This may be somewhat difficult but not impossible. The effort will be valuable as models will be found to inspire youth.

Victor Lowenfeld recognized the need of such self-actualizing or self-development, and his life's work was a result of efforts to meet this need. One of his early students, John Biggers, now an outstanding artist and teacher, told in an interview how Lowenfeld first came to the United States from Austria as a "scholar refugee" to teach psychology at Hampton

7. Personal interview with R. C. Gorman, 1974.

Figure 9.8   R. C. Gorman. *Corn Mother*. Lithograph, 30 x 22 inches. Reproduced by courtesy of R. C. Gorman.

Figure 9.9   Fritz Scholder. *Indian with Blanket*. Acrylic 80 x 68 inches. Reproduced by courtesy of Fritz Scholder and from the collection of the Elaine Horowitch Gallery.

Institute, a college for Black youth in Virginia. Biggers had come to Hampton from North Carolina to study plumbing, but a night course with Lowenfeld caused him to change to an art major.

Biggers had become interested in art while in high school even though no courses in art were offered. While working as a janitor he copied pictures from the New York Times on the boiler room walls. He had never known or heard of a Black artist and had never entertained the thought of becoming an artist.

Lowenfeld taught psychology his first year at Hampton, but being an artist in Europe and having worked with children, art education was his "springboard." Lowenfeld couldn't understand why no courses in the visual arts were offered at Hampton. He saw Black people active in music, dance, and theatre, but not the visual arts, and wondered why. He raised the question with President Howe, who was White, as had been all the early presidents of Hampton. President Howe explained that, "these people are not interested in the visual arts," but Lowenfeld could not accept this answer. He asked for and was given the opportunity to offer a night class in drawing, for no credit, to see if there would be any volunteers.

Hampton Institute consisted of 750 Black students at that time and 700 of them showed up for this night class without credit, Biggers claimed with a smile. This is how the art program at Hampton Institute began. In the second year Lowenfeld initiated a major in the field of art. His was a one-man department at the time, which offered drawing, painting, and sculpture. Although Lowenfeld was not skillful on the potter's wheel, he found a student who was good in carpentry and showed him a picture of a potter's wheel. This student, Joe Gillard, built the wheel and taught himself to throw pots through Lowenfeld's instruction, although the instructor, Lowenfeld, could not throw a pot. This is how the ceramics instruction began. He also managed to get an old printing press and taught printmaking to the students.

Biggers relates that it was partly due to Lowenfeld that Charles White and Elizabeth Catlett came to Hampton, with the help of a Rosenwald Fellowship. This was the first opportunity that Hampton students

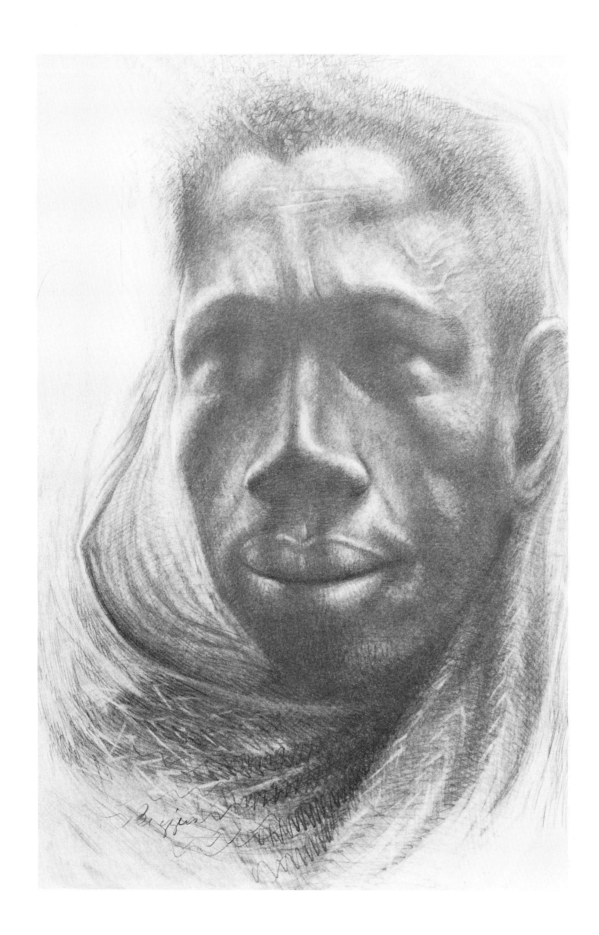

Figure 9.11 Hughie Lee-Smith. *Outing.* Reproduced by courtesy of Hughie Lee-Smith.

had to see Black professional artists at work. White's fellowship was to paint a mural with the subject matter that dealt with the contributions of Black people to the United States. During the first semester, due to the lack of a studio, White developed his plan for the mural in the classroom and used students as models in portraying Black historical figures. They were able to observe his work in progress. Seeing the expert draftsmanship of Charles White discouraged many students who felt they should drop art because they thought it would be impossible to attain his level of skill in drawing.

Elizabeth Catlett, who was then married to Charles

White, taught sculpture and provided another dimension of understanding for the students. She gave an additional source of inspiration and provided a model which was at the same time both Black and female. "At this time," Biggers recalls, "Viktor Lowenfeld, Charles White, Betty Catlett, and Joe Gillard were teaching art at Hampton, and it was a wonderful experience."[8]

During the interview, Biggers relates that Lowenfeld while teaching at Hampton wrote his definitive work, *Creative and Mental Growth,* which was not published until later when he went to Pennsylvania State College. Illustrations in the original text came from the art department at Hampton Institute, Phoenix High School of Hampton,

Figure 9.10 John Biggers. *Man.* Conté crayon, 24 x 36 inches. Reproduced by courtesy of John Biggers and from the collection of the Golden State Mutual Life Insurance Company.

8. Taped interview with John Biggers, 1970.

Virginia, and from classes of Victor D'Amico in New York, illustrations that have been omitted or replaced in later editions.

Biggers credits Charles and Betty White as having a tremendous influence on him and his work, because they were models to whom he could relate both aesthetically and ethnically. Another influence for him later was that of Hale Woodruff and the Atlanta school. He called the art department of Atlanta University, headed by Hale Woodruff, the first vital school of Black art in the United States and used it as a model when he established the art department at Texas Southern University in Houston. At this school Biggers said his objective was, "to develop a community center of art which meant training teachers and craftsmen, and to create a shrine for our neighborhoods."[9]

In the process of creating this shrine, Biggers, with his colleagues and his students painted murals and created monuments on the campus and in the community. These works have been inspired by a number of models: Woodruff's *Amistad Mutiny* mural at Talladega College, Alabama; Aaron Douglas' murals at Fisk University, Tennessee; and New York's Harlem YMCA and Public Library branch; Alston's Harlem Hospital mural, works produced by the WPA project artists, and the Mexican muralists, Rivera, Siqueros, and Orozco. "Our objective was to create for the people, in the imagery that the people could 'dig'." He seemed somewhat irritated that the "young turks" today are raving about their search for identity, "which is not a new thing for many of us, which the young leaders do not realize." This comment was in reference to the many murals painted on walls during the explosive 1960s which affirmed the dignity and respect of the Black person. "On the other hand," he reflected, "it is good that these young artists discover for themselves something of their own heritage, that

they learn how to learn more of the black cultural history, the black artist, and of the black movement in America."[10]

When asked his interpretation of "Black art" he replied,

"to me it means that people must reflect their struggle, their history, their search for their own identity and spiritual values. They must affirm their own life. If we think in terms of identification of the average American, and especially 'moral' identification, we get into the essence of what Black Art is. I think that the black man represents a moral identity, to a great extent, of this country. And this is what we want to affirm in art. To me, this is what Black Art is."[11]

The success of the "shrine" that John Biggers went to Texas to build, the quality of his own work, and the quality of his teaching can be judged by the recognition each has received, and this has been considerable. The affirmation to which John Biggers refers was admirably summed up by Germaine Greer on a television talk show in which she commented, "To be without a tradition is about the most degrading thing an artist faces."

No person is an island standing alone in today's world. Like the trunk and branches of a tree, one stems from the roots and soil in which he or she is planted. Ancestors and environment make the basic ingredients, but will, choice, self-discipline, and self-determination leading to self-actualization coupled with accident, luck, and uncontrolled forces determine the ultimate outcome of one's success.

9. Ibid.
10. Ibid.
11. Ibid.

Bibliography

Art West Associated North, Inc. *New Perspectives in Black Art.* Oakland: Oakland Museum, 1968.

Ashton-Warner, Sylvia. *Teacher.* New York: Bantam, 1963

———. *Spinster.* New York: Simon & Schuster, 1971.

Association for Supervision and Curriculum Development, N.E.A. *Perceiving Behaving Becoming: A New Focus for Education.* Washington, D.C.: Yearbook, 1962.

Bearden, Romare and Green, Carroll. *The Evolution of Afro-American Artists: 1800-1950.* New York: City University, 1967.

Bennett, Gwendolyn. *Exhibition of Works by Prominent Negro Artist.* New York: Harlem Community Art Center. Federal Art Project, W.P.A., 1939.

Bennett, Jr., Lerone. *Before the Mayflower.* Baltimore: Penguin Books, 1961.

———, ed. "The Emancipation Proclamation." *Ebony Magazine.* Special issue, September, 1963.

Biggers, John. *Ananse.* Austin: University of Texas Press, 1962.

———. "Interview." Art Department, Texas Southern University, Houston, Texas, 1970.

Biobaku, S. I. *Yoruba Art in German and Swiss Museums.* Ibadan: Yoruba Historical Research Scheme, 1958.

Black Academy of Arts and Letters, Inc. *Conference to Assess the State of Black Arts and Letters in the U.S.* Chicago: Johnson Publishing Company and National Endowment for the Arts, 1972.

Boyce, George A. *Learning and Living at IAIA.* Santa Fe, New Mexico: United States Department of Interior, Bureau of Indian Affairs, Albuquerque Area Institute of American Indian Arts, 1965.

Braithwaite, E. R. *To Sir with Love.* Englewood Cliffs, N.J.: Prentice-Hall, Inc., 1959.

Breeskin, Adelyn. *William H. Johnson 1901-1970.* Washington: Smithsonian Institution Press, 1971.

Brown, Sterling, ed. *The Negro Caravan.* New York: The Dryden Press, 1941.

Bushnell, Don. "Black Arts for Black Youth." *Saturday Review,* 18 July 1970: pp. 43-46.

Carroll, Keven. *Yoruba Religious Carving: Pagan and Christian Sculpture in Nigeria and Dahomey.* New York: Praeger, 1967.

Chapman, Abraham, ed. *Black Voices.* New York: New American Library, Mentor, 1968.

Chase, Judith Wragg. *Afro-American Art and Craft.* New York: Van Nostrand Reinhold Co., 1971.

Church, Peggy Pond, ed. *The Writer's Reader.* Santa Fe: Institute of American Indian Arts, 1967.

Clark, Kenneth. *Civilisation: A Personal View.* New York: Harper and Row, 1970.

Clarke, John Henrik. "Slave Revolt in the Caribbean." *Black World,* February 1973, pp. 12-25.

Cole, Herbert M. "Mbari Is Life." *African Arts* 2, no. 3 (Spring 1969): 8-17.

Columbus Historical Society. *Zoar.* Columbus: 1952.

Conant, Howard, *Seminar on Elementary and Secondary School Education in the Visual Arts.* Cooperative Research Project No. V003. New York: New York University Press, 1965.

Cushman, Bernard. *This Is the One.* Phoenix: Truth Publications, 1970.

Damas, Leon G. "Negritude in Retrospect." *Curricular Approaches to African and African-American Studies.* Edited by E. W. Eko. Greensboro: Six Institutions' Consortium, 1970, pp. 1-12.

Davidson, Basil. *The African Slave Trade*. Boston: Little, Brown and Company, 1961.

———. *The Lost Cities of Africa*. Boston: Little, Brown and Company, 1959.

Davis, R. T. *Native Arts of the Pacific Northwest*. Stanford: Stanford University Press, 1949.

Davis, Ronald W. "Negro Contributions to the Explorations of The Globe." *The Negro Impact on Western Civilization*. Edited by Joseph S. Roucek and Thomas Kiernan. New York: Philosophical Library, 1970.

Delange, Jacqueline. *The Art and Peoples of Black Africa*. Translated by Carol F. Jopling and others. New York: E. P. Dutton and Co., Inc., 1974.

De Roo, Peter. *History of America Before Columbus*. Philadelphia: J. B. Lippincott Company, 1900.

Diop, Cheikh A. *The African Origins of Civilization: Myth or Reality*. Edited and translated by Mercer Cook. New York: Lawrence Hill and Co., 1974.

Delury, George E. ed. *The World Almanac*. New York: Newspaper Enterprise Association, 1973.

Dockstader, Fredrick. *Indian Art in America*. Greenwich, Conn.: New York Graphic Society, 1961.

Donaldson, Jeff. CONFABA (Conference on the Functional Aspects of Black Art). Evanston: Northwestern University, 1970.

Douglas, Fredrick and D'Harnoncourt, Rene. *Indian Art of the United States*. New York: Museum of Modern Art, 1941.

Douglas, Fredrick. *Indian Masks*. Denver: Denver Museum, 1940.

Dover, Cedric. *American Negro Art*. Greenwich, Conn.: New York Graphic Society, 1960.

Du Bois, W. E. B. *The World and Africa*. New York: International Publishers, 1965.

Ewing, Roberta A. "Fritz Scholder." *The 74th Western Annual*. Edited by Lewis Story. Denver: Denver Museum, 1973, p. 48.

Fax, Elton. *17 Black Artists*. New York: Dodd Mead and Company, 1971.

Feder, Norman. *American Indian Art*. New York: Harry N. Abrams, Inc., 1965.

Fine, Elsa H. *The Afro-American Artist*. New York: Holt, Rinehart and Winston, 1973.

Forbes, Jack D. *Afro-Americans in the Far West. A Handbook for Educators*. Berkley: Far West Laboratory for Educational Research, n.d.

Forge, Anthony, ed. *Primitive Art and Society*. London: Oxford Press, 1973.

Foster, Marcus. *Making Schools Work*. Philadelphia: Westminster Press, 1971.

Fowler, Charles B., ed. *Urban Culture Awareness May Save Our Skins*. Washington, D.C.: Music Educators National Conference, 1970.

Freyre, Gilberto. *The Masters and the Slaves*. New York: Alfred A. Knopf, 1946.

Glaeser, William. "Art Concepts of Reality, and the Consequences of the Celebration of Peoples." *Studies in Art Education* 15, no. 1 (Washington: National Art Education Association, 1973): 34-43.

Grant, Joanne, ed. *Black Protest: History, Documents and Analysis*. Greenwich: Fawcett Publications, Inc., 1968.

Greene, Carrol. "The Afro-American Artist." *The Humble Way* 7, no. 3 (Houston, 1968): 10-15.

———. *Romare Bearden: The Prevalence of Ritual*. New York: The Museum of Modern Art, 1971.

Grigsby, J. Eugene, Jr. "Art Education at Carver High School." *Art Education*. NAEA Journal, May, 1954.

———. "Celebration of Peoples." Honolulu: NAEA Conference Program, 1972.

———. *Encounters*. Charlotte: Johnson C. Smith University Exhibit Catalog, 1968.

———. Taped interview with John Biggers, 1970.

———. Taped interview with R. C. Gormon, 1974.

———. Taped interview with Hughie Lee Smith, 1970.

Grossman, Emery. *Art and Tradition: The Jewish Artist in America*. New York: Thomas Yoseloff, 1967.

Grube, Ernst J. *The World of Islam*. New York: McGraw-Hill.

Hansberry, William Leo. "Indigenous African Religions." *Africa Seen by American Negroes*. Edited by John A. Davis. Paris: Presence Africaine, 1958.

Hayes, Floyd W. "The African Presence in America Before Columbus." *Black World* 22, no. 9. (Chicago: Johnson Publishing Company, 1973): 4-11.

Hitti, Phillip K. *The Arabs: A Short History*. Princeton: Princeton University Press, 1949.

Holm, Bill. *Northwest Coast Indian Art: An Analysis of Form*. Seattle: University of Washington Press, 1965.

Howard University. *Ten Afro-American Artists of the Nineteenth Century*. Washington, 1967.

Hughes, Langston. *The Big Sea*. New York: American Century Series, Hill and Wang, 1940.

———. "The Twenties: Harlem and Its Negritude." *African Forum* 1, no. 4 (1966): 11-20.

Inverarity, R. Bruce. *Art of the Northwest Coast.* Berkeley: University of California Press, 1950.

Jahn, Janheinz. *Muntu.* New York: Grove Press, Inc., 1961.

Kamarck, Edward, ed. "The Arts and the Black Revolution." *Arts in Society* 5, no. 11 (Madison: University of Wisconsin Press, 1968).

Kent, R. K. "Palmares: An African State in Brazil." *Journal of African History* 6 (1965), p. 161-176.

Krickus, Richard J. "The White Ethnics: Who Are They and Where Are They Going?" *City* 5, no. 3, May/June 1971, p. 25.

Kolber, Jane. "An Investigation of Navajo Culture with Implications for Navajo Art Education." Master's Thesis. Arizona State University, 1974.

Law, R.C.C. "The Heritage of Oduduwa: Traditional History and Political Propaganda Among the Yoruba." *Journal of African History* 4: 207-222.

Lawrence, Harold G. "African Explorers of the New World." *The Crisis,* June/July, 1962.

Leiris, Michel and Delange, Jacqueline, *African Art.* New York: Golden Press, 1968.

Lewis, Samella and Waddy, Ruth. *Black Artists on Art.* Los Angeles: Contemporary Crafts, Inc., vol. 1, 1969, vol. 2, 1971.

Lincoln, C. Eric. *The Negro Pilgrimage in America.* New York: Bantam Path Finder Edition, Bantam Books, 1967.

Linton, Ralph. *The Tree of Culture.* New York: Alfred A. Knopf, 1955.

Lipman, Jean and Winchester, Alice. *The Flowering of American Folk Art.* New York: Viking Press with Whitney Museum of Art, 1974.

Locke, Alaine. "Up Till Now." *The Negro Artist Comes of Age.* Albany: Albany Institute of History and Art, 1945.

———. "The Art of the American Negro (1851-1940)." *American Negro Exposition.* Chicago, 1940.

———. *The Negro in Art.* New York: Hacker Art Books, 1968.

Lowenfeld, Vicktor. *Creative and Mental Growth.* New York: Macmillan Co., 1950.

Lowenfeld, Vicktor and Lambert, Brittain W. *Creative and Mental Growth.* 5th ed. New York: The Macmillan Co., 1970.

Montgomery, E. J. *California Black Craftsmen.* Oakland, California: Mills College Art Gallery, 1970.

———. "New Perspectives in Black Art, an Exhibition." Oakland: Oakland Museum and Art-West Associated/North, Inc., 1968.

Murphey, Judith and Gross, Ronald. *The Arts and the Poor: New Challenge for Educators.* Washington: U.S. Department of Health, Education, and Welfare, 1968.

New, Lloyd. *Cultural Difference as a Basis for Creative Development.* Santa Fe: Institute of American Indian Arts, 1967.

Nicolaides, Kimon. *The Natural Way to Draw.* Boston: Houghton Mifflin Co., 1941.

Nyerere, Julius K. "Speech to the Congress." *The Black Scholar,* July/August, 1974.

Ohio Historical Society. *Zoar: An Ohio Experiment in Communalism.* 1952.

Orleans, Peter, and Ellis, William R., Jr., eds. *Race, Change, and Urban Society.* Beverly Hills: Sage Publications, 1971.

Ott, Carlos. "Influencia Arabica Na Arte Baiana." *Afro-Asia,* no. 10-11. Salvador: Centro de Estudos Afro-Orientals, 1970.

Otto, John S. and Burns, Augustus M. "Black and White Cultural Interaction in the Early Twentieth Century South: Race and Hillbilly Music." *Phylon* 36 (Atlanta University, 1974): 407-417.

Pal, Pratapaditya, ed. *Islamic Art.* Los Angeles County Museum, 1973.

Paz, Octavio. *Labrynth of Solitude: Life and Thought in Mexico.* Translated by Lysander Kemp. New York: Grove Press, 1962.

Pearson, Ralph M. *The New Art Education.* New York: Harper and Brothers, 1941.

Porter, James A. *Modern Negro Art.* New York: Dryden Press, 1943.

———. "The Negro in American Art." Los Angeles: California Arts Commission, 1966.

Purifoy, Noah and others. *Mixed Media.* Los Angeles: Plantin Press, 1961.

Quirarte, Jacinto. "The Art of Mexican-America." *Humble Way* 9, no. 2 (Houston: Humble Oil and Refining Company, 1970).

———. *Mexican American Artists.* Austin: University of Texas Press, 1973.

Reinert, Jeanne. "Secrets of the People of the Jaguar." *Science Digest.* September, 1967.

Robinson, Armstead L., ed. *Black Studies in the University.* New York: Bantam Books, 1969.

Rogers, Carl. *On Becoming a Person*. Boston: Houghton Mifflin Co., 1961.

Rose, Hanna T. *The Role of the Arts in Meeting the Social and Educational Needs of the Disadvantaged*. New York: Brooklyn Museum, 1967.

Santa Clara County Office of Education. *Creating from Many Cultures*. Santa Clara County, California, 1970.

Schuyler, George S. *Black No More*. New York: Macualay Co., 1931.

Scottsdale National Indian Arts Council, Inc. *Tenth Scottsdale National Indian Arts Exhibition*. Scottsdale, Arizona, 1971.

Seldis, Henry. "Introduction." *Dimensions of Black*. Jehanne Tielhet, ed. La Jolla: La Jolla Museum of Art, 1970.

Shaker Inspirational Drawings. An exhibition of the collection of Dr. and Mrs. Edward D. Andrews by Smith College Museum of Art, Robert O. Parks, Director, 1960.

Silverman, Ronald H. and Hoepfner, Ralph. *Developing and Evaluating Art Curricula Specifically Designed for Disadvantaged Youth*. Final Report Project Number 6-1657, Contract Number OEC-4-6-061657-16410. Washington, D.C.: United States Department of Health, Education and Welfare Office of Education, Bureau of Research, March 1969.

"Spiral." An Exhibition of Black Artists, East Coast. New York, 1965.

Taylor, Edward K. *New Black Artists*. New York: Harlem Cultural Council and Urban Center of Columbia University, 1969.

Temples, R. P. *The Bantu Philosophy*. Paris: Presence Africaine, 1948.

Teilhet, Jehanne, ed. *Dimensions of Black*. La Jolla, Calif.: La Jolla Museum of Art, 1970.

Thompson, Robert Farris. "African Influence on the Art of the United States." *Black Studies in the University*. Edited by A. L. Robinson, C. G. Foster, and D. H. Oglice. New York: Bantam Books, 1969.

Turk, Rudy. "Rip Woods." *The 74th Western Annual*. Denver: Denver Museum, 1973.

U.S. Commission on Civil Rights. *Counting the Forgotten: The 1970 Census Count of Persons of Spanish Speaking Background in the United States*. Washington, D.C., April 1974.

Von Hagen, Victor W. *The Ancient Sun Kingdoms of the Americas*. New York: The World Publishing Co., 1957.

Von Wuthenau, Alexander. *The Art of Terracotta Pottery in Pre-Columbian Central and South America*. New York: Crown Publishers, Inc., 1970.

Waters, Frank. *Masked Gods: Navaho and Pueblo Ceremonialism*. New York: Ballantine Books, 1950.

Wescott, Joan. *Yoruba Art in German and Swiss Museums*. Ibaden: Yoruba Historical Research Scheme, 1958.

White, Anne Terry. *George Washington Carver*. New York: Random House, 1953.

White, Walter. *A Man Called White: The Autobiography of Walter White*. Bloomington, Ind.: Indiana University Press, 1948.

Whiton, Louis C. "Under the Power of the Gran Cadu." *Natural History, Journal of the American Museum of Natural History*. New York, 1971.

Wiener, Leo. *Africa and the Discovery of America*. Philadelphia: Innes and Sons, 1922.

Willis, John Ralph. "The Spread of Islam." *The Horizon History of Africa*. Edited by Alvin M. Joseph, Jr., American Heritage Publishing Co., 1971, pp. 136-175.

Wingert, Paul S. *American Indian Sculpture*. New York: J. J. Augustin, 1949.

Zorbaugh, Harvey. *The Gold Coast and the Slum*. Chicago: University of Chicago Press, 1929.

Index

Gwathmey, Robert, 6

Hadith, Moslem law, 76
Hallgarten Prize, 119
Hampton Institute, 132, 135
Hansberry, Leo, 68, 69, 72
Harlem, 107
　　Globetrotters, 37, 39
　　poets, 109
　　Renaissance, 93, 94, 108, 110
Harleston, Edwin, 4, 101
Harmon Foundation, 4, 95
Harper's Ferry, 87
Harvey, Fred, collection, 17
Hauptmann, Gerhart, 91, 92
Hawthorne, Charles, 119
Hayden, Palmer, 110
Hayes, Floyd, 44, 72
Heard Museum, 19, 22
Henry, Patrick, 93
Heritage, 127, 132
　　African, 37, 114
　　Jewish, 77
　　Mexican, 12
　　respect for, 127
Herodotus, 62
Heye Foundation of Indian Arts, 17
hierarchy of arts, 126
Hill, Esther, 6
Hill, Joan, 21
Hinds, Patrick, 21, **22**
Hindu, 51
Hines, Felrath, 5, 9
History of Rhode Island, 117
Hitler, Adolph, 39
Hogarth, William, 91, 92
Holbein, Hans, 62
Hollingsworth, Alvin, 5, 9
Hope, Dr. John, 110
Hopi, 48
　　capture of, 66
　　creation myth, 78
　　resistance by, 83
Horse, John, Indian chief, 96
hostilities between religious groups, 51
Houser, Alan, **2, 12,** 21, **26, 112**
Howe, Oscar, **19,** 21, 129
Hughes, Langston, 101, 103, 107,
　　108, 109
Humble Way Magazine, 16
Humphrey, Hubert, 14
Hunt, Richard, 4
Hurston, Zora Neal, 109
hyphenated-Americans, 47

Ibeji society, 74
idols, idolatry, 66, 79, 80; Aztec, 96
Idowu, Dr. Baloji, 74
Ifa society, 74
Ikhnaton, 61

Ille Ife, 73
Illinois Bell Exhibition, 6
immigrants
　　European, 51, 107
　　illegal, 37
India, 44
Indian Art of the United States, 19
Indians, Blackfeet, x
Indians, Native American, 23
　　description of whites as pink, ix
　　difficulty adjusting to urban
　　　centers, 125
　　misnamed by Columbus, 44
Ingram, Jerry, **28**
Ingram, Zell, 4
Inquisition in Mexico, 46
INSEA International Society of
　　Education through Art, 33
insolence, 35
Institute of American Indian Art, 21,
　　128
integrated communities, 124
integrity, aesthetic, 124
intercontinental art, 121, 122
international art, 79, 120
intrinsic value in art, 91
Inverarity, Bruce, 19
Iowa State College, 37
ironwork in New Orleans, 76
Iroquoian tribes, 83
Isabella (Sojourner Truth), 87
Isis, Egyptian deity, 61
Islam, 73
　　influence in the New World, 75, 76
Israelites, 85
Italian city states, 120

Jackson, Andrew, 96
Jahn, Janheinz, 47
Jamestown, landing of first slaves, 46
Java, 47
jazz, 126
Jefferson, Bob, 9
Jefferson, Thomas, 67
Jesuits, 66, 83
Jewish, xii, 42, 51, 77
Jews, barred from Louisiana, 67
Jiminez, Luis, 16
Job, slave artist, 116, 117
John Herron Institute of Art, 95, 110
Johnson, Hall, 109
Johnson, Herbert F., Museum, 6
Johnson, James Weldon, 109
Johnson, J. P., 110
Johnson, Sargent, 4, 101
Johnson, William H., 4, **115, 116,
　　118,** 119
Johnston, Joshua, 4, **113,** 114
Jones, Lois Mailou, 9, **10, 61, 69,** 101
Joseph, Cliff, 9

Judaism, xi, 76, 77
Judie, Edward, **31**
Kabotie, Fred, 21
Kaffarians, 47
Kafir, 47
Kambinda, Raquel, **69, 75**
Kandinsky, Wassily, 123
Kaprow, Allan, 23
Karamu House, 109
Karolik, Maxim, 114
Kino, Father, 66
Kiowa, 48
Kirchner, Ernst, 6
Kissi, 47
Kobayashi, Michio, **2**
Kolber, Jane, 77
Kollwitz, Kathe, 91, 92
Koran, 76
Kriskus, Richard, 125
Kuczynski (population statistics), 46
Kwakiutl, 48, 121

La Jolla Museum, 5
Lamp Black exhibition, 6, 9,
language, 51, 52, 53
language, Sea Island, 52
La Salle, Robert, 66
Lautreamont, 103
law, Islamic, 76
Law, John, 67
Lawrence, Jacob, 4, 6, **32, 43, 48, 86,**
　　94, 96, 128
Lazard, Luener, **35**
Lee-Smith, Hughie, 4, 129, 135, **135**
Le Moyne, Pierre, 67
Leris, Michael, 40
Lero, Etienne, 103
letter from Texas art teacher, xi
Lewis, Edmonia, 126
Lewis, Elma, School of Fine Arts, 6,
　　128
Lewis, Norman, 4, 5
Lewis, Samella, 3, **52**
Liberia, 47
Links, Inc., The National, 6
Linton, Ralph, 53, 59
Lipchitz, Jacques, 6
Lipman, Jeanne, 113, 114
Lloyd, Tom, 9
Locke, Alain, 3, 4, 109
Loloma, Charles, 21
Lopez, Michael, 16
Los Caprichos, 91
Louis XIV, 63, 67
Louis, Joe, 37, 39
Louisiana, 66, 67
L'Ouverture, Toussaint, 80
Love, George, 6
Lowenfeld, Viktor, 12, 132, 133, 135

Luks, George, 119
Luther, Martin, 62, 91

Machitoches, 67
Majors, William, 5
Malaya, 47
Malevich, Kasimir, 123
Mali, 76
Mali King, Abubakari II, 43
Mande, Mandingo, 46
Mansa Musa, 43
Martel, Charles, 62
Martinez, Maria, 21
masks, 19
Masked Gods, 19
massacre, Boston, 85
Matisse, Henry, 6, 37
Mayhew, Richard, 5, 9
Mazlow, Abraham, 127
McCullough, Geraldine, **101**
McFee, June, ix, x, xii
McFee, Malcom, x
McKay, Claude, 93, 103, 109
Mead, Margaret, ix
Mecca, 76
Medellin, Octavio, 16
Melle, 67
melting pot, 23, 51, 124
Menonites, 83
mestizo, 40, 81
Mexican-American, xi, 1, 9, 12, 13,
    14, 15, 16, 21, 23, 39, 47, 107,
    114
Mexican school of art, 91
Mexico, 47
Michelangelo, 36
Micumba, 74
Miller, Earl, 5
Mills College, 9
Miracle of the Roses, 99
missionaries
    attempts to convert Indians, 77
    Franciscan, 66
    French, 67
missions, 66
Mobile, 67
models, 36
    as heroes, 37
    for image building, 117
    lack of, 126
Modern Negro Art, 3, 117
Modigliani, Amedeo, 6
Mohawk, 81
Mondrian, Piet, 120, 123
monolithic, 40
Montgomery, Evangeline, 9
Moore, Henry, 6
Moorehead, Scipio, 114
Moors, defeat of, 62, 65
Moravia, 63

mosaic murals, 62
Moses, 61
Moslem, 40, 51, 75, 76
Motley, Archibald, 101
Mozambique, 47
Muhammed, 75, 76
mulligan stew, 23, 127
Murray, Charles, 1
Museum of the American Indian,
    Heye Foundation, 17
Museum of Fine Arts, Boston, 6
Museum of Modern Art, 52, 123, 128
music
    blues, 93
    ethnic, 126
    spirituals, 93
Music Educators Journal, 30
Muslim, Black, 75
mythology
    Greek, 62
    Hopi, 78
    Navajo, 79
    Pueblo, 79

NAACP, 57
Nagos, 46
Napoleon, 67
    Napoleonic wars, 63
National Academy of Design, 119
National Art Education Association,
    33
    Pacific Region, 23, 26
National Center of Afro-American
    Artists, 6
National Conference on Poverty, 14,
    23
Native American religion, 77
Native Art of the Pacific Northwest,
    19
Navajo, 19, 48
    organization of space, 77
Navajo Trail of Tears, 83
Navarro, Fernando, 17
Nazis, 91
Neal, Robert, 12
negritude, 99, 103, 108, 109
Negro in Art, The, 3
neighborhoods, ethnic, 125
Neimeyer, Oscar, 123
Neri, Manuel, 16
New Black Artists, 6
New, Lloyd, 21, 128
New Orleans ironworks, 117
New York University, 110
Nicolaides, Kimon, 39
Nigeria, 76
Niño, Pedro, 46
Noble & Sissle, 109

noble savage image, 83
Nunez, David, **14**, 17
Nupe, 46

Oba, 73, 75
Obatala, 73, 75
Oduduwa, 73
Ogboni society, 74
Ogun society, 47
Okeechobee, battle of, 96
Oklahoma Art Center, 22
O'Leary, Diane, **78**
Omolu, 74, 75
Oneida, 81
Oni, 73, 75
Onondaga, 81
Oriental, xii, 37
Orishas, Yoruba, xi, 47, 73
    costumes, 75
    possessed by, 85
    societies, 74, 75
Orishifunfun society, 74
Oroke society, 74
Orozco, Clemente, 15, 91, 136
Ortiz, Ralph, 16
Oshun, 47
Osiris, 61
Osumare, 74
Our Lady of the Conception, 47
outbreaks, slave, 96
Outterbridge, John, 9, **92, 95**
Overstreet, Joseph, 6
Owens, Jesse, 37, 39

Pacific Arts Association, 23
    Portland Convention, 1
Paladin, David Chethlahe, **20**, 21, **24**
Palimino, Ernesto, 16
Pan African Congress, 109
Park, Dr. Mungo, 67, 68
parties, house rent, 110
Pearson, Ralph, 12
Pechstein, Max, 6
Pena, Amado, 16
Phi Beta Kappa, 110
Philbrook Art Center, 22
Phoenix High School, Hampton, Va.,
    135
Picasso, Pablo, 6, **7**, 37, **87**, 91, 123
Pilgrims, 126
Pima, 48
Pippin, Horace, 4, 6
plots, slave, 85
poem, epic, *History of New Mexico*,
    66
poetry, Creole, 103
poets, Harlem, 108, 109
Poitiers, Moors defeated at, 62
Polish-American, 47
Pollard, Fritz, 39